Holy Moly! Top 50 Egg-Free Recipes Volume 15

David J. Patel

Copyright: Published in the United States by David J. Patel/ © DAVID J. PATEL

Published on June, 24 2021

All rights reserved. No part of this publication may be reproduced, stored in retrieval system, copied in any form or by any means, electronic, mechanical, photocopying, recording or otherwise transmitted without written permission from the publisher. Please do not participate in or encourage piracy of this material in any way. You must not circulate this book in any format. DAVID J. PATEL does not control or direct users' actions and is not responsible for the information or content shared, harm and/or actions of the book readers.

In accordance with the U.S. Copyright Act of 1976, the scanning, uploading and electronic sharing of any part of this book without the permission of the publisher constitute unlawful piracy and theft of the author's intellectual property. If you would like to use material from the book (other than just simply for reviewing the book), prior permission must be obtained by contacting the author at cookbook@lowpotassiumrecipes.com

Thank you for your support of the author's rights.

Content

50 AWESOME EGG-FREE RECIPES 4

1. Almond Pea Pesto Pasta 4
2. Amazing Veggie Stoup 4
3. Anchovy And Caper Dressing 5
4. Antipasto "Dip" 5
5. Apricots With Blue Cheese 6
6. Artichoke Salad With Oranges 6
7. Basil Butter Orzo 7
8. Budget Savvy Sang Choy Bow 7
9. Cabbage With Celery And Water Chestnuts 8
10. Cabbage And Basmati Rice Casserole 8
11. Cajun Barbecued Shrimp 9
12. Char Siu Pork Tortillas 9
13. Chicken With Basil And Red Peppers 10
14. Chickpeas And Fennel With Rice 10
15. Cinnamon Cream Cheese Apples 11
16. Cinnamon Sorbet 11
17. Curried Spinach Onion Rice 12
18. Easy Healthy Weeknight Tuna Tomato Skillet 12
19. Easy Peasy Tzatziki 13
20. French Creole Cod 13
21. Frosted Coffee 14
22. Grilled Halibut With Tomato Basil Salsa .. 14
23. Grilled Portabella And Arugula Burgers ... 15
24. Healthy Avocado Cucumber Ranch 15
25. Hearty Beef Barley Pilaf 16
26. Husband Wife Super Easy Sauteed Chicken 16
27. Japanese Fried Chicken (Tori Karaage) 17
28. Microwave Cajun Crumb Chicken 17
29. Mixed Berry Sauce To Be Enjoyed With Meat 18
30. Morg Kebab (Iranian Skewered Chicken) 18
31. Pesto Orzo With Peas 19
32. Potted Stilton With Port And Walnuts 19
33. Quick Soba Stir Fry With Tofu 20
34. Salmon, Avocado And Grapefruit 20
35. Selderijsoep Michigan Dutch Celery Soup 21
36. Sherried Baby Squash 21
37. Slow Cooker Irish Stew 22
38. Smoked Fish And Fresh Fruit 22
39. Southwestern Beef Chili With Corn 23
40. Spaghetti Agli E Olio 23
41. Spicy Garlic Grilled Shrimp 24
42. Spicy Rice Filled Eggplant 24
43. Sweet Chilli Chicken Salad (21 Day Wonder Diet: Day 17) 25
44. Theodore Kyriakou's Fricassee Of Green Dandelion Leaves 25
45. Tilapia And Shrimp En Papollote 26
46. Tofu Dorowat 27
47. Vegan Marinade (Marinated Tofu) 27
48. Vegetable Stir Fry With Cashew Chilli 28
49. Very Cheesy Macaroni And Cheese 28
50. Whole Grain Sesame Bread 29

INDEX 31
CONCLUSION 35

50 Awesome Egg-Free Recipes

***

1. Almond Pea Pesto Pasta

Serving: 16 serving(s) | Prep: 10mins | Cook: 7mins

Ingredients

- 1 lb penne or 1 lb other short pasta
- 2 (10 ounce) packages frozen peas (thawed)
- 1/2 cup blanched almond
- 1 -1 1/2 teaspoon salt
- 1 lemon (zest and juice)
- 1/4 cup olive oil

Direction

- Boil a large pot of salted water, and cook pasta according to directions. When there are about 2 minutes left on pasta, add one of the packages of peas.
- Drain the pasta except for about 1 cup of water, and then return the pasta and water to the pot.
- In a food processor grind the almonds.
- Now add the lemon zest and juice to the almonds, along with the remaining package of peas, and the salt. Process again. You might have to scrape it down the sides after a minute to make sure it mixes evenly. If the taste is too strong, add more peas.
- Add the olive oil and process again.
- Now add the sauce to the pasta, tossing it well and adding water as needed. Season with salt and pepper.
- Enjoy!

Nutrition Information

- Calories: 186.1
- Sodium: 187.4
- Sugar: 2.1
- Total Carbohydrate: 29
- Total Fat: 6.4
- Fiber: 5.4
- Cholesterol: 0
- Protein: 5
- Saturated Fat: 0.8

2. Amazing Veggie Stoup

Serving: 6-10 serving(s) | Prep: 20mins | Cook: 30mins

Ingredients

- 30 ounces stewed tomatoes
- 1 zucchini, chopped
- 1 medium onion, chopped
- 4 carrots, chopped
- 1 cup green beans, chopped
- 1/2 cup spinach, chopped
- 1 -2 sweet potato, chopped
- 1 cup chicken stock
- 1 teaspoon ground chipotle chile pepper
- 1 teaspoon chili pepper flakes
- 4 cups spaghetti squash

Direction

- Roast zucchini, onion, carrots, and sweet potatoes for 45.
- In large pot or crockpot simmer tomatoes and chicken stock. Add chipotle pepper and pepper flakes.
- Add roasted veggies when done. Simmer for 30minutes.

- Roast squash while the rest is simmering. When done drag a fork through squash to separate strands.
- Serve Sauce/stoup over spaghetti squash.

Nutrition Information

- Calories: 130.9
- Protein: 4.6
- Cholesterol: 1.2
- Saturated Fat: 0.3
- Sodium: 453.9
- Fiber: 4.7
- Sugar: 11.8
- Total Carbohydrate: 28.4
- Total Fat: 1.4

3. Anchovy And Caper Dressing

Serving: 4 serving(s) | Prep: 10mins

Ingredients

- 2 tablespoons lemon juice
- 5 tablespoons olive oil
- 1 teaspoon fresh ground black pepper
- 6 anchovy fillets, pounded to a coarse paste
- 1 tablespoon capers, chopped

Direction

- Mix together all ingredients.
- Salt should not be needed because of the anchovies.

Nutrition Information

- Calories: 165.5
- Total Fat: 17.5
- Sodium: 284.4
- Fiber: 0.2
- Cholesterol: 5.1
- Saturated Fat: 2.5
- Sugar: 0.2

- Total Carbohydrate: 1.1
- Protein: 1.9

4. Antipasto "Dip"

Serving: 10 serving(s) | Prep: 5mins

Ingredients

- 2 (14 ounce) canswhole artichoke hearts (drained)
- 2 cloves garlic
- 1 (12 ounce) can roasted red peppers (drained)
- 2/3 cup packed fresh flat-leaf parsley
- 1/4 cup extra virgin olive oil
- 3 tablespoons fresh lemon juice
- 3 tablespoons red wine vinegar
- 2/3 cup oil-cured black olive (remove pits)
- 1 teaspoon salt
- 1/2 teaspoon fresh ground pepper

Direction

- Place artichoke hearts and garlic in food processor.
- Pulse on and off until roughly chopped.
- Add the rest of the ingredients and continue to pulse until finely chopped (but not to the point of minced or puréed) Allow to stand refrigerated for at least an hour for the flavors to marry.
- Serve with crusty bread or crudités.

Nutrition Information

- Calories: 107.6
- Total Carbohydrate: 11.7
- Cholesterol: 0
- Protein: 3.3
- Total Fat: 6.6
- Sugar: 0.9
- Sodium: 1041.8
- Fiber: 5.2
- Saturated Fat: 0.9

5. Apricots With Blue Cheese

Serving: 36 apricot bites | Prep: 5mins | Cook: 2mins

Ingredients

- 18 small fresh apricots
- 1/4 cup olive oil
- 1 tablespoon freshly squeezed lime juice
- salt freshly ground black pepper
- 1/4 lb blue cheese

Direction

- Cut apricots in half and remove pits, place in large bowl.
- Mix oil and lime juice together and season with salt and pepper, pour over apricots and toss gently.
- Place apricot halves, cut-side-up, on cookie sheets.
- Cut blue cheese into small pieces and place in the centre of each apricot.
- No more than one hour before serving place under preheated broil for one to two minutes or just until cheese softens.

Nutrition Information

- Calories: 32.9
- Total Fat: 2.5
- Saturated Fat: 0.8
- Sodium: 44.2
- Fiber: 0.3
- Total Carbohydrate: 2.1
- Sugar: 1.6
- Cholesterol: 2.4
- Protein: 0.9

6. Artichoke Salad With Oranges

Serving: 4 serving(s) | Prep: 25mins | Cook: 25mins

Ingredients

- 4 artichokes (about 2 pounds)
- 1 lemon, halved crosswise
- 4 oranges
- 6 radishes, thinly sliced
- 12 kalamata olives
- 2 tablespoons extra virgin olive oil
- 1/2 teaspoon sweet paprika
- salt, to taste

Direction

- Fill a large pan with water and bring to a boil. Add the artichokes and half of the lemon to the pan. Cover and cook the artichokes until they are barely tender, about 20 to 25 minutes. Drain and set aside to cool.
- When artichokes are cool enough to handle pull off the leaves and cut out the fuzzy chokes. Slice the hearts into bite size wedges and squeeze the other half of lemon over the hearts, set aside. Peel and section the oranges discarding the seeds and white pith in a large bowl.
- When ready to serve, alternate orange sections and artichoke wedges on individual plates. Garnish with radish slices, olives and a mixture of the olive oil and lemon juice that will be drizzled over the salad. Sprinkle with paprika and salt, serve immediately.

Nutrition Information

- Calories: 203.8
- Saturated Fat: 1.2
- Sugar: 12.4
- Total Carbohydrate: 32.9
- Protein: 5.9
- Total Fat: 8.6
- Sodium: 239.1
- Fiber: 11.9
- Cholesterol: 0

7. Basil Butter Orzo

Serving: 8-10 serving(s) | Prep: 10mins | Cook: 15mins

Ingredients

- 1 lb orzo pasta
- 1 red bell pepper
- 1 yellow bell pepper
- 1/2 cup butter
- 1 1/2 cups basil leaves, lightly packed
- 2 garlic cloves
- 1/4 lb cherry tomatoes, halved
- 1/4 lb feta cheese, crumbled
- 1 (4 ounce) jar capers, drained

Direction

- Bring 3 qt. of water to a boil in a large pot. Add orzo and cook until pasta is just tender to bite, ten minutes. Drain orzo and return to pan.
- Meanwhile, finely chop bell peppers, set aside.
- In a food processor, combine butter, basil and garlic. Add this mixture to orzo in pan. Stir over medium-low heat until butter is melted and pasta is hot.
- Stir in peppers, tomatoes, cheese and capers, Pour onto a rimmed platter and serve hot, warm or at room temperature.

Nutrition Information

- Calories: 372.2
- Sodium: 668.9
- Fiber: 3.6
- Sugar: 2.7
- Protein: 10.9
- Total Fat: 15.7
- Saturated Fat: 9.6
- Total Carbohydrate: 47.7
- Cholesterol: 43.2

8. Budget Savvy Sang Choy Bow

Serving: 6 Budget-savvy Sang Choy Bow, 6 serving(s) | Prep: 10mins | Cook: 15mins

Ingredients

- 6 iceberg lettuce leaves
- 1 tablespoon vegetable oil
- 1 -2 garlic clove, crushed
- 1 red capsicum
- 500 g beef sausages (16 ounces)
- 1/4 cup plum sauce
- 1/4 cup sweet chili sauce
- 1 tablespoon soy sauce
- 400 g brown lentils, drained (just under 13 ounces)
- 4 spring onions, thinly sliced
- sea salt, to taste
- fresh ground black pepper, to taste
- extra spring onion, thinly slices, to garnish
- lime wedge, to serve

Direction

- Trim the lettuce leaves into cup shapes.
- Heat the oil in a non-stick pan; add the garlic and capsicum; cook, stirring occasionally, until almost soft.
- Snip one end of the sausages with the kitchen scissors; squeeze out 1cm (1/2 inch) lengths of meat from each sausage into the pan; cook, stirring, until browned and cooked through. Reserve the rest of the sausages for use in another dish.
- Add the combined sauces, brown lentils and spring onions; stir over the heat until the lentils are hot; season with salt and pepper.
- To serve, divide the sausage mixture among the leaves; garnish with extra onions; serve with lime wedges.

Nutrition Information

- Calories: 494.3

- Total Fat: 17.6
- Sugar: 5.8
- Cholesterol: 38.3
- Saturated Fat: 5.5
- Sodium: 1475.8
- Fiber: 21.9
- Total Carbohydrate: 52.4
- Protein: 31.1

9. Cabbage With Celery And Water Chestnuts

Serving: 4-6 serving(s) | Prep: 15mins | Cook: 45mins

Ingredients

- 1 large onion, sliced
- 1 green bell pepper, cut into large pieces
- 3 stalks celery, chopped
- 2 tablespoons canola oil
- 4 -6 cups cabbage, cut into large bite sized pieces
- 1 cup water
- 1 (8 ounce) can sliced water chestnuts, drained
- salt and black pepper, to taste

Direction

- Sauté the onion, bell pepper and celery in the oil until translucent but not brown.
- Add cabbage and water, cover and simmer for 25 to 30 minutes.
- Add water chestnut slices to cabbage.
- Season with salt and pepper.
- Cook 10 more minutes.

Nutrition Information

- Calories: 132.9
- Total Fat: 7.2
- Cholesterol: 0
- Saturated Fat: 0.6
- Sodium: 44.3
- Fiber: 4.5

- Sugar: 6.8
- Total Carbohydrate: 16.9
- Protein: 2.3

10. Cabbage And Basmati Rice Casserole

Serving: 8 serving(s) | Prep: 15mins | Cook: 50mins

Ingredients

- 1 cup basmati rice
- 1 small cabbage
- 4 tablespoons margarine
- 2 stalks celery
- 4 garlic cloves
- 2 vegetable bouillon cubes or 2 chicken bouillon cubes
- 2 cups water

Direction

- Preheat oven to 400.
- Shred cabbage in food processor.
- Process garlic and celery in food processor until chopped VERY small.
- Melt butter in skillet and add rice, cabbage, celery and garlic.
- Stir until rice is lightly browned and veggies are tender.
- Pour into 1 1/2 quart casserole dish.
- Sprinkle bouillon cubes over the top.
- Pour two cups of water over all.
- Cover with foil and bake for 50 - 60 minutes or until rice is tender.

Nutrition Information

- Calories: 161.3
- Saturated Fat: 1.1
- Sodium: 93.6
- Fiber: 3
- Sugar: 3.6
- Total Carbohydrate: 23.7

- Protein: 3.4
- Cholesterol: 0
- Total Fat: 6.5

11. Cajun Barbecued Shrimp

Serving: 4 serving(s) | Prep: 0S | Cook: 10mins

Ingredients

- 1 teaspoon cayenne pepper
- 1 teaspoon fresh ground black pepper
- 1 teaspoon salt
- 1/4 teaspoon crushed red pepper flakes
- 1 teaspoon paprika
- 1 teaspoon dried rosemary
- 1/2 teaspoon dried thyme
- 1/2 cup unsalted butter
- 1 lb shrimp, shelled and deviened
- 1 cup beer
- 1/2 cup shrimp stock
- 2 teaspoons lemon juice
- 1 tablespoon cornstarch

Direction

- In a large skillet, melt the butter.
- Add the cayenne, black pepper, salt, red pepper, paprika, rosemary, and thyme.
- Cook until bubbly.
- Add the shrimp and coat with the butter mixture.
- Cook 1 minute.
- Add the beer and shrimp stock and cook for 2 - 4 minutes.
- Mix the lemon juice and cornstarch.
- Add cornstarch mixture to thicken and cook for 1 minute more.

Nutrition Information

- Calories: 355.2
- Saturated Fat: 15
- Fiber: 0.7
- Total Carbohydrate: 5.4
- Cholesterol: 281.9
- Protein: 24.4
- Total Fat: 24.5
- Sodium: 841.6
- Sugar: 0.2

12. Char Siu Pork Tortillas

Serving: 10 Char Siu Pork Tortillas, 10 serving(s) | Prep: 20mins | Cook: 10mins

Ingredients

- 500 g pork fillets, thinly sliced
- 240 g char siu sauce
- 2 tablespoons hoisin sauce
- 1 tablespoon vegetable oil
- 250 g mini tortillas
- 2 green spring onions, thinly sliced
- 1 carrot, cut into matchsticks
- 1 red capsicum, thinly sliced
- 10 toothpicks

Direction

- Place the pork and sauces in a medium bowl; toss to coat; cover and refrigerate for 2 hours, or overnight; drain the pork, reserving the marinade.
- Heat the oil in a hot wok; add the pork in two batches; stir-fry for 5 minutes or until it is just cooked through; remove from the wok and cover to keep warm while cooking the second batch.
- Place the reserved marinade in a small saucepan; bring to the boil and gently simmer for 5 minutes; remove from the heat and cover to keep warm.
- Heat tortillas according to the packet directions; divide the pork among the tortillas; top with onions, carrot and capsicum; roll up tightly to enclose the filling; secure with a toothpick.

- Serve the tortillas with the warm marinade as a dipping sauce.
- NOTE: Char siu is a sweet and rich Chinese barbecue sauce.

Nutrition Information

- Calories: 167.6
- Sugar: 2.2
- Total Carbohydrate: 15.8
- Cholesterol: 31.6
- Total Fat: 5.6
- Sodium: 241.1
- Fiber: 1.4
- Saturated Fat: 1.4
- Protein: 12.9

13. Chicken With Basil And Red Peppers

Serving: 2 serving(s) | Prep: 10mins | Cook: 20mins

Ingredients

- 3 tablespoons vegetable oil
- 6 garlic cloves (cut into thin slices)
- 4 chopped scallions
- 1 red bell pepper (seeded and diced)
- 1 lb chicken breast (diced)
- 3 tablespoons fish sauce
- 2 teaspoons dark soy sauce
- 1 teaspoon sugar
- 24 Thai basil

Direction

- Heat oil in wok or frying pan over medium heat.
- Add garlic, scallions, red pepper and stir fry 5 minutes.
- Add chicken and cook until done.
- Stir in fish sauce, soy sauce, and sugar and cook until sauce begins to become thick (about 5-10 minutes).
- Stir in basil leaves and cook 5 minutes or just until leaves are wilted.
- Garnish with fresh basil if desired and enjoy.

Nutrition Information

- Calories: 630.5
- Saturated Fat: 8.7
- Sodium: 2571.7
- Fiber: 2.2
- Sugar: 6.5
- Total Carbohydrate: 12.2
- Cholesterol: 145.3
- Total Fat: 41.7
- Protein: 51

14. Chickpeas And Fennel With Rice

Serving: 2 serving(s) | Prep: 0S | Cook: 30mins

Ingredients

- 1 medium fennel bulb, chopped in one inch pieces
- 1 (19 ounce) can chickpeas
- 1 big garlic clove, diced with centre removed
- 2 tablespoons olive oil
- 1/8 teaspoon garam masala
- fennel, tops chopped
- salt and pepper
- 1/2 cup rice
- 1 cup water

Direction

- Soak rice in pot for ten minutes in enough water to cover. When ten minutes are up, rinse the rice and add 1 cup fresh water. Cover and bring to a boil, then set on low heat to simmer for 8-9 minutes.
- While rice cooks, chop fennel bulb and put in pan with olive oil. Cook on medium heat until fennel begins to soften.

- Add chopped garlic, chickpeas, salt and pepper.
- When rice is finished cooking, turn off burner under rice and leave, covered, for ten minutes more (makes it fluffy).
- Add garam masala to chickpeas and fennel for remaining five minutes of cooking, while the rice is sitting, and add fresh fennel tops (the feathery parts) near the end of cooking (just to warm them up).
- Serve side by side on big plates, and enjoy!

Nutrition Information

- Calories: 653.9
- Total Fat: 17.1
- Saturated Fat: 2.3
- Sodium: 869.6
- Total Carbohydrate: 108.6
- Cholesterol: 0
- Fiber: 16.2
- Sugar: 0
- Protein: 18.1

15. Cinnamon Cream Cheese Apples

Serving: 6 serving(s) | Prep: 15mins | Cook: 15mins

Ingredients

- 6 apples
- 2/3 cup red cinnamon candies
- 2 cups water
- 3 ounces cream cheese
- 2 tablespoons milk
- 1 teaspoon lemon juice
- 1/3 cup pitted dates, chopped
- 1 (8 ounce) can crushed pineapple, drained
- 2 tablespoons chopped walnuts

Direction

- Peel and core apples.
- Mix candies and water in a saucepan and cook until candies are dissolved. Add apples. Simmer, uncovered until tender, about 15 minutes, turning them over half way through the cooking process. Chill in syrup for several hours.
- In a small bowl, blend cream cheese, milk, lemon juice, dates, pineapple and nuts. Drain apples on rack. Stuff center of apples with cream cheese mixture.
- To serve, place an apple on a serving plate. Drizzle with the syrup.

Nutrition Information

- Calories: 190.9
- Saturated Fat: 3.4
- Sodium: 48
- Sugar: 26.2
- Total Carbohydrate: 33.4
- Protein: 2.4
- Fiber: 4.6
- Cholesterol: 16.3
- Total Fat: 7

16. Cinnamon Sorbet

Serving: 8 , 8 serving(s) | Prep: 20mins | Cook: 3hours

Ingredients

- 5 cups water
- 1 1/4 cups granulated sugar
- 1 -2 cinnamon stick (based on your taste-buds)
- 2 tablespoons cold water
- 1 tablespoon cornstarch
- 2 teaspoons lemon juice

Direction

- Boil the five cups of water with cinnamon until it has color, flavor, and reduces to four cups total in liquid.
- Add the sugar and let it boil for five minutes.

- Dissolve the corn starch into the cold water and stir until completely dissolved. Now add to the previous preparation and let it cook for five minutes over a medium high heat.
- Remove pan from the heat, and let it cool down a little. Add the lemon juice.
- Strain the preparation into a freezer proof container.
- Once cold, put the mixture in the freezer. Before it gets completely frozen, stir the sorbet so that it does not get very hard (approximately every 30-45 minutes). Repeat this two or three times, until the sorbet is ready to enjoy. In my freezer it took three times but I still tried a fourth and did not see a huge difference in texture.

Nutrition Information

- Calories: 125
- Saturated Fat: 0
- Sodium: 5
- Fiber: 0
- Sugar: 31.2
- Total Carbohydrate: 32.2
- Cholesterol: 0
- Total Fat: 0
- Protein: 0

17. Curried Spinach Onion Rice

Serving: 6 serving(s) | Prep: 10mins | Cook: 20mins

Ingredients

- 1/4 peanut oil
- 2 brown onions, cut into slices
- 1 tablespoon curry powder
- 2 cardamom pods, bruised
- 1 cinnamon stick
- 4 whole cloves
- 2 bay leaves
- 1 1/2 cups basmati rice
- 3 cups chicken stock
- 100 g baby spinach leaves
- 1/2 cup sliced almonds, toasted
- 1 long red chili, thinly sliced

Direction

- Heat oil in a large saucepan over moderate heat. Cook and stir onion for 8-10 minutes or until golden. Transfer to a plate. Set aside.
- Reheat pan; add curry powder, cardamom, cinnamon, cloves and bay leaves. Cook and stir for 1 minute. Add rice; stir to combine. Add stock; cover with a lid. Bring to boil. Reduce heat; cook for 15 minutes or until liquid is absorbed. Remove from heat. Stand for 5 minutes. Using a fork, separate grains. Remove cardamom pods, cinnamon stick, cloves and bay leaves. Stir in spinach until it wilts. Season with salt.
- Spoon rice into a large serving bowl. Top with onion, almonds, and chili.

Nutrition Information

- Calories: 281.4
- Saturated Fat: 1
- Sodium: 189.7
- Fiber: 3.8
- Cholesterol: 3.6
- Total Fat: 6.9
- Sugar: 4.3
- Total Carbohydrate: 46.4
- Protein: 9.3

18. Easy Healthy Weeknight Tuna Tomato Skillet

Serving: 4 cups, 4 serving(s) | Prep: 5mins | Cook: 10mins

Ingredients

- 3 tablespoons olive oil
- 2 -3 garlic cloves, chopped

- 1 (14 ounce) candied chili-ready tomatoes
- 1/8 cup pickled jalapeno pepper
- 1/8 teaspoon cayenne pepper
- 1/4 teaspoon garlic salt
- salt and pepper
- 2 (6 ounce) cans tuna fish, drained
- 1 (14 ounce) can great northern beans, drained

Direction

- Heat olive oil in skillet on medium-high heat, add garlic and sauté for about a minute.
- Add tomatoes, jalapenos, cayenne pepper, garlic salt, and salt and pepper to taste. Bring to a simmering boil, reduce heat to medium.
- Stir in tuna and mix thoroughly.
- Gently stir in Great Northern beans and heat through. Serve alone or over rice with a salad and garlic toast.

Nutrition Information

- Calories: 283.1
- Total Fat: 11.2
- Sodium: 360.5
- Fiber: 5.6
- Total Carbohydrate: 17.1
- Cholesterol: 25.5
- Saturated Fat: 1.7
- Sugar: 0.1
- Protein: 28.3

19. Easy Peasy Tzatziki

Serving: 1 1/2 cups, 6 serving(s) | Prep: 15mins

Ingredients

- 250 g Greek yogurt
- 2 garlic cloves, minced (or finely chopped)
- 1 lebanese cucumber, grated, drained
- 1 lemon, juice of
- 2 teaspoons salt
- salt and pepper, to season

Direction

- Mix the cucumber with the salt in a small container and put aside in the fridge for at least 10 minutes.
- Squeeze cucumber to drain it of any excess liquid.
- Combine the yogurt, garlic, lemon juice and cucumber in a small container and mix well.
- Season with salt and pepper.
- Place in the fridge for at least 1 hour to allow flavours to develop.
- Serve.

Nutrition Information

- Calories: 11
- Total Carbohydrate: 2.8
- Protein: 0.4
- Total Fat: 0.1
- Saturated Fat: 0
- Sodium: 776.4
- Fiber: 0.3
- Sugar: 1
- Cholesterol: 0

20. French Creole Cod

Serving: 4-6 serving(s) | Prep: 10mins | Cook: 15mins

Ingredients

- 1 lb cod
- 2 teaspoons olive oil (and extra for brushing on the baking sheet)
- 2 teaspoons Dijon mustard
- 1/2 teaspoon salt
- 1/2 teaspoon creole seasoning, your favorite
- 1 tablespoon lemon juice, feshly squeezed
- chopped fresh parsley

Direction

- Preheat oven to 400°F Line a rimmed baking sheet with foil and brush very lightly with olive oil.
- Mix the olive oil, mustard, salt and Creole seasoning together.
- Brush the spice mixture evenly over the fish and place on the prepared sheet.
- Bake for 15 to 17 minutes or until the fish flakes easily with a fork.
- To serve:
- Drizzle with the lemon juice and sprinkle parsley over the fish. Serve immediately.

Nutrition Information

- Calories: 115.3
- Sodium: 380.3
- Sugar: 0.1
- Cholesterol: 48.7
- Protein: 20.3
- Total Fat: 3.1
- Saturated Fat: 0.5
- Fiber: 0.1
- Total Carbohydrate: 0.4

21. Frosted Coffee

Serving: 2 serving(s) | Prep: 5mins

Ingredients

- 1 cup crushed ice
- 1/2 cup vanilla ice cream
- 1/4-1/3 cup coffee liqueur
- 1/2 teaspoon instant coffee

Direction

- In blender, combine ice, ice cream, liqueur and instant coffee.
- Cover and blend at high speed about 20 seconds or until smooth.
- Pour into chilled glasses.

Nutrition Information

- Calories: 180.6
- Total Fat: 4.1
- Saturated Fat: 2.5
- Sugar: 18.8
- Protein: 1.4
- Sodium: 34.1
- Fiber: 0.2
- Total Carbohydrate: 19.9
- Cholesterol: 15.8

22. Grilled Halibut With Tomato Basil Salsa

Serving: 2 serving(s) | Prep: 10mins | Cook: 10mins

Ingredients

- 1 tablespoon extra virgin olive oil
- 1 tablespoon balsamic vinegar
- 1 garlic clove, minced or pressed
- 1/8 teaspoon kosher salt
- 1/8 teaspoon ground black pepper
- 1 medium tomatoes, cored seeded and diced
- 1/2 ounce basil leaves, sliced into ribbons (about 5 large leaves)
- 8 ounces halibut fillets
- salt and pepper

Direction

- In a non-reactive bowl, whisk together the oil, vinegar, garlic, salt and pepper.
- Add the tomatoes and basil, stirring gently to combine. Set aside while you cook the fish.
- Preheat your grill to medium high.
- If your fish has skin on it, season the flesh side with salt and pepper. If it has no skin, place the fish on a folded piece of aluminum foil, large enough to hold the fish in one flat layer, coated with cooking spray. Season with salt and pepper.
- Place the fish on the grill, skin/foil side down. Cook until the fish flakes with a fork or is

barely opaque in the middle. It should still look a little wet in the centre.
- Remove the flesh from the skin (I just leave the skin on the grill and burn it off) or the foil, and place on a serving platter. Stir the salsa, then drizzle over the fish. Serve immediately.

Nutrition Information

- Calories: 208.9
- Total Fat: 8.8
- Sodium: 208.3
- Total Carbohydrate: 4.5
- Cholesterol: 68.6
- Protein: 26.7
- Saturated Fat: 1.4
- Fiber: 0.9
- Sugar: 2.9

23. Grilled Portabella And Arugula Burgers

Serving: 4 serving(s) | Prep: 10mins | Cook: 20mins

Ingredients

- 1/2 cup fat-free mayonnaise
- 2 teaspoons Dijon mustard
- 6 teaspoons minced fresh rosemary
- 1 garlic clove, minced
- nonstick vegetable oil cooking spray
- 4 large portabella mushrooms, stems trimmed
- 2 tablespoons olive oil
- arugula
- whole grain buns

Direction

- Mix mayonnaise, mustard, 2 teaspoons rosemary and garlic in small bowl.
- Spray grill rack with nonstick spray, then prepare barbecue (medium heat). Brush mushrooms all over with olive oil. Sprinkle each with 1 teaspoon rosemary, then salt and pepper. Grill until tender, about 10 minutes per side.
- Spread mayonnaise mixture over buns. Place mushrooms and arugula on bun bottoms. Cover with bun tops.

Nutrition Information

- Calories: 108
- Sugar: 3.8
- Total Carbohydrate: 8.9
- Sodium: 273.6
- Fiber: 2.1
- Protein: 2.4
- Total Fat: 7.9
- Saturated Fat: 1.1
- Cholesterol: 3.2

24. Healthy Avocado Cucumber Ranch

Serving: 1 cup, 2 serving(s) | Prep: 5mins

Ingredients

- 1 large avocado
- 1/2 cucumber
- 1/2 cup Greek yogurt
- 1 (1 ounce) package ranch dip mix
- black pepper

Direction

- Blend all ingredients in a blender until smooth. Adjust ingredients to get the desired thickness and taste. Dump on your salad or enjoy with chips!

Nutrition Information

- Calories: 204.2
- Total Fat: 17.8
- Saturated Fat: 2.6
- Sodium: 9.9

- Sugar: 2
- Total Carbohydrate: 13
- Cholesterol: 0
- Protein: 2.9
- Fiber: 8.5

- Total Carbohydrate: 28.9
- Total Fat: 9.2
- Saturated Fat: 2.5
- Sodium: 635
- Fiber: 6.8

25. Hearty Beef Barley Pilaf

Serving: 6 serving(s) | Prep: 30mins | Cook: 1hours30mins

Ingredients

- 2 tablespoons olive oil
- 1 cup onion (chopped)
- 2 -3 garlic cloves
- 1 lb stewing beef
- 1 (32 ounce) box beef broth
- 1/2 cup red wine
- 1/2 cup water
- 1 cup barley
- barley, is not gluten free
- 2 bay leaves
- ground black pepper
- 1 -2 dash Worcestershire sauce
- 1 cup cherry tomatoes (halved, or a can of chopped tomatoes)
- 8 ounces sliced mushrooms (crimini best)
- 1 cup cabbage, 1 inch dice

Direction

- In a heavy Dutch oven, sauté onion garlic in olive oil. Add beef and brown. Add everything else, bake at 350 for 1.5 hours or till everything is tender. I also added some herbs, and some dry falafel mix.

Nutrition Information

- Calories: 300.3
- Cholesterol: 48.4
- Protein: 23.9
- Sugar: 3.3

26. Husband Wife Super Easy Sauteed Chicken

Serving: 2 serving(s) | Prep: 10mins | Cook: 10mins

Ingredients

- 1 1/2 boneless skinless chicken breasts
- sea salt fresh black pepper
- 1/4 cup all-purpose flour
- 2 1/2 tablespoons salted butter
- 1 -2 tablespoon fresh parsley, chopped
- lemon wedge

Direction

- Wash and pat dry the chicken breasts, then trim off fat.
- Put them between two pieces of plastic wrap and pound out evenly to a ½ inch thickness with a mallet.
- Season generously with sea salt and fresh cracked pepper (both sides).
- Dust lightly with flour (both sides) and shake off excess just before adding to pan.
- Melt 2 ½ tablespoons butter in large sauté pan over med-high heat.
- Add chicken breasts and cook for about 3 minutes on each side. (You'll know when it's done when breasts are browned sufficiently on both sides.) Remove and allow to rest for a few minutes.
- Sprinkle with parsley, squirt with lemon wedges, and serve.

Nutrition Information

- Calories: 282.2

- Sodium: 161.1
- Sugar: 0.1
- Total Fat: 15.7
- Saturated Fat: 9.4
- Fiber: 0.5
- Total Carbohydrate: 12.1
- Cholesterol: 89.5
- Protein: 22.3

27. Japanese Fried Chicken (Tori Karaage)

Serving: 4 serving(s) | Prep: 10mins | Cook: 10mins

Ingredients

- 70 ml soy sauce
- 70 ml sake
- 1 teaspoon garlic, crushed
- 1 teaspoon ginger, crushed
- 1/2 cup potato flour
- 500 g chicken thighs, cut into bite sized pieces
- canola oil, for frying

Direction

- Mix together soy, sake, garlic and ginger. Add chicken to soy mixture and marinate for at least an hour. Heat oil in medium size saucepan. Drain extra liquid from chicken and coat with potato flour. Cook chicken in oil in small batches until golden brown and floating on the surface of the oil. Allow to rest for five minutes and serve.

Nutrition Information

- Calories: 373.5
- Cholesterol: 105
- Protein: 25.4
- Sodium: 1296.1
- Saturated Fat: 5.4
- Fiber: 1.4
- Sugar: 1.1

- Total Carbohydrate: 19.2
- Total Fat: 19.2

28. Microwave Cajun Crumb Chicken

Serving: 6 serving(s) | Prep: 10mins | Cook: 15mins

Ingredients

- 2 tablespoons Dijon mustard
- 1 tablespoon honey
- 1 tablespoon tomato paste
- 1/2 cup crumbled corn flakes
- 1/2 teaspoon poultry seasoning
- 1/2 teaspoon paprika
- 1/2 teaspoon celery salt
- 1/4 teaspoon salt
- ground red pepper
- 2 1/2 lbs broiler-fryer chickens, skinned cut up

Direction

- In a small bowl, combine mustard, honey and tomato paste.
- On waxed paper combine corn-flake crumbs with poultry seasoning, paprika, celery salt, salt and red pepper.
- Coat chicken pieces one at a time in mustard/honey mixture, then roll in seasoned crumbs.
- In a 13"x9" baking dish, arrange chicken with thicker pieces toward the edges.
- Cook chicken, covered loosely with waxed paper, on High 11 to 13 minutes (until juices run clear), rearranging pieces once.
- Let stand 5 minutes before serving.

Nutrition Information

- Calories: 432.2
- Sodium: 323.6
- Sugar: 3.6
- Saturated Fat: 8.2

- Total Carbohydrate: 6
- Cholesterol: 141.9
- Protein: 35.7
- Total Fat: 28.7
- Fiber: 0.4

29. Mixed Berry Sauce To Be Enjoyed With Meat

Serving: 4 serving(s) | Prep: 0S | Cook: 10mins

Ingredients

- 1 orange, juice of
- 1 bay leaf
- 3 tablespoons red currant jelly
- 150 g mixed berries (fresh or frozen, if frozen then defrost beforehand)
- 1/2 tablespoon of fresh mint
- 1/2 teaspoon brown sugar
- 1 tablespoon balsamic vinegar
- juices from cooked meat

Direction

- Cook the meat that is going to be served in a pan and then remove it and set aside to rest, covering with foil to retain the heat.
- Add the orange juice, bay leaf, redcurrant jelly, berries and sugar to the meat juices left in the pan from cooking the meat and boil the mixture for 3-4 minutes.
- Lower the heat and simmer uncovered for another 5 minutes until the fruit is soft.
- Remove the bay leaf, stir in the balsamic vinegar, mint and season with salt and pepper.
- Spoon over the meat and serve immediately while hot.

Nutrition Information

- Calories: 90.8
- Cholesterol: 0
- Saturated Fat: 0

- Sodium: 6.5
- Total Carbohydrate: 23
- Sugar: 10.4
- Protein: 0.7
- Total Fat: 0.1
- Fiber: 1

30. Morg Kebab (Iranian Skewered Chicken)

Serving: 6 serving(s) | Prep: 5mins | Cook: 5mins

Ingredients

- 1 1/2 kg chicken, jointed
- 3 onions, grated
- 3 lemons, juice of
- 60 g ghee or 60 g butter, melted

Direction

- Keeping the pieces large, remove as much meat as possible from the joints and cut it into pieces.
- Combine the onion and lemon juice in a bowl, add the chicken and marinate for at least 2 hours.
- Drain and combine the butter or ghee with the marinade.
- Thread the meat onto lightly greased skewers and cook over glowing coals or - on a preheated grill - for 5 minutes or until the meat is tender.
- Baste with the marinade and turn once.
- Serve with melted butter, and Borani Esfenaj (Iranian Spinach Salad) and Chilau (Iranian Rice) (posted separately).

Nutrition Information

- Calories: 443.6
- Sodium: 108.6
- Fiber: 0.9
- Total Carbohydrate: 7.6

- Cholesterol: 139.7
- Protein: 28.9
- Total Fat: 32.9
- Saturated Fat: 12.8
- Sugar: 2.9

31. Pesto Orzo With Peas

Serving: 5 serving(s) | Prep: 10mins | Cook: 12mins

Ingredients

- 1 cup orzo pasta, uncooked
- 1 1/2 cups frozen peas
- 1/4 cup pesto sauce
- 1/3 teaspoon salt
- pepper

Direction

- In a large saucepan, cook orzo as directed on the package, adding the peas during the last 4 to 6 minutes of cooking time, cook until tender.
- Drain excess liquid. Add pesto and toss gently to coat. Sprinkle with salt and pepper. Serve.
- Makes 5 (3/4 cup) servings.

Nutrition Information

- Calories: 157.9
- Sodium: 204.9
- Sugar: 2.9
- Total Carbohydrate: 31
- Protein: 6.6
- Saturated Fat: 0.1
- Cholesterol: 0
- Total Fat: 0.7
- Fiber: 2.9

32. Potted Stilton With Port And Walnuts

Serving: 4-6 serving(s) | Prep: 10mins

Ingredients

- 8 ounces Stilton cheese
- 3 ounces butter
- 2 tablespoons port wine
- 1 pinch ground mace
- 2 ounces toasted walnut halves
- melted butter, to pour over the top

Direction

- To make the potted Stilton, simply mash the Stilton in a bowl, add the softened butter, the mace and port and continue to stir together well.
- (Traditional potted cheese recipes tend to use unclarified butter, presumably because cheese, especially when it is aided by alcohol, needs less protection from spoilage than meat.).
- Pack into ramekins or an attractive ceramic pot/s. Melt a little butter and pour over the top of the cheese to form a thin seal.
- Scatter the walnuts over the top press them in slightly, then leave it to set.
- Refrigerate for up to a week. Serve after dinner with crackers or hot, toasted rye bread, with a ripe pear alongside. Alternatively, try as a sandwich filling on wholemeal bread, augmented by plenty of crisp salad leaves to cut through the richness of this delicious potted cheese!

Nutrition Information

- Calories: 457.2
- Saturated Fat: 22.4
- Sugar: 1.2
- Protein: 14.5
- Total Carbohydrate: 4.3
- Cholesterol: 88.2
- Total Fat: 42.8
- Sodium: 914.4

- Fiber: 1

33. Quick Soba Stir Fry With Tofu

Serving: 4 serving(s) | Prep: 10mins | Cook: 20mins

Ingredients

- 8 ounces uncooked soba noodles
- 2 tablespoons toasted sesame oil
- 1 lb extra firm tofu, drained and cubed
- 1 cup shiitake mushroom, sliced
- 1 cup warm water
- 2 garlic cloves, finely minced
- 1 cup scallion, finely chopped
- 1 1/2 tablespoons soy sauce, to taste (divided)

Direction

- Cook soba as package directs, rinse and drain.
- Set aside.
- Soak mushrooms in water for 5 minutes; drain.
- Heat oil in a skillet and sauté the garlic for 1 minute.
- Add the mushrooms and sauté 2-3 minutes.
- Add the tofu cubes and half of the soy sauce; sauté 3-5 minutes.
- Mix in the cooked soba, remaining soy sauce and scallions.
- Sauté another 5 minutes or so until the soba is hot.
- Serve.

Nutrition Information

- Calories: 345.4
- Sodium: 847.6
- Sugar: 1.4
- Total Carbohydrate: 47.2
- Total Fat: 12
- Saturated Fat: 2
- Fiber: 1.8
- Cholesterol: 0

- Protein: 18.8

34. Salmon, Avocado And Grapefruit

Serving: 4 serving(s) | Prep: 10mins | Cook: 15mins

Ingredients

- 2 large ripe avocados
- 2 ripe grapefruits, peeled
- 4 (150 g) fresh salmon fillets, with skin
- 2 tablespoons lemon juice
- 4 tablespoons extra virgin olive oil, plus
- 1 tablespoon extra extra virgin olive oil, for frying
- salt and pepper

Direction

- Whisk the lemon juice, olive oil, salt and pepper in a large bowl to make a dressing.
- Peel and core the avocado and cut the flesh in to chunks, dropping them directly into the dressing.
- Trim any white pith from the grapefruit. Cut into small segments and add to the dressing along with any extra juices. Toss lightly and chill for 10 minutes or so.
- Heat the remaining oil in a heavy pan and cook the salmon, skin – side down, until the skin is crisp and the flesh turns pale pink. Turn and cook on the other side, leaving the salmon soft and pink in the middle.
- Place the salmon, skin side up on serving plates and top with a big spoonful of avocado and grapefruit.
- Spoon the juices around the salmon and serve.

Nutrition Information

- Calories: 555.8
- Protein: 33.1
- Total Fat: 39.9

- Saturated Fat: 5.8
- Total Carbohydrate: 20.6
- Cholesterol: 78
- Sodium: 109.3
- Fiber: 8.1
- Sugar: 1

35. Selderijsoep Michigan Dutch Celery Soup

Serving: 6 serving(s) | Prep: 10mins | Cook: 10mins

Ingredients

- 2 cups celery, diced (stalks and leaves)
- 1 onion, finely minced
- 1 1/2 cups water, boiling
- 3 tablespoons butter
- 4 tablespoons flour
- 3 cups milk
- 1 1/2 teaspoons salt
- 1/8 teaspoon black pepper

Direction

- Cook celery and onion in boiling water for ten minutes.
- In another pan, melt the butter; add flour and blend.
- When flour and butter are fully incorporated, add milk and cook, stirring constantly until thick.
- Add the cooked celery and onion with the cooking liquid to the white sauce.
- Season to taste with salt and pepper.
- Serve hot.

Nutrition Information

- Calories: 160.5
- Total Fat: 10.3
- Saturated Fat: 6.5
- Sodium: 710.8
- Sugar: 1.4

- Cholesterol: 32.3
- Protein: 5
- Fiber: 0.9
- Total Carbohydrate: 12.5

36. Sherried Baby Squash

Serving: 4 serving(s) | Prep: 5mins | Cook: 15mins

Ingredients

- 1 quart baby squash, mixed (like zucchini, yellow and pattypan)
- 3 tablespoons butter
- 1 sweet onion, diced
- 2 tablespoons sherry wine (the good stuff, not cooking sherry)
- 2 teaspoons fresh thyme, chopped
- garlic salt
- fresh ground black pepper

Direction

- Wash and slice the squash into 1/2 inch pieces.
- In a large frying pan, melt the butter over medium high heat. Add the onion and sauté for 4-5 minutes, or until it is beginning to caramelize and stick to the bottom of the pan.
- Deglaze the pan with the sherry, scraping up the brown bits. When the sherry has cooked down to a thick liquid, add the squash, thyme and some garlic salt. Toss to coat with butter and onions. Spread squash out over the bottom of the pan so that they can brown, about 1-2 minutes.
- When one side is lightly browned, flip squash over to brown on other side. When browned, add pepper and toss. Serve hot.

Nutrition Information

- Calories: 136.6
- Total Fat: 8.9

- Sodium: 81.3
- Fiber: 1.8
- Cholesterol: 22.9
- Protein: 1.8
- Saturated Fat: 5.5
- Sugar: 4
- Total Carbohydrate: 7.5

37. Slow Cooker Irish Stew

Serving: 4 serving(s) | Prep: 15mins | Cook: 3hours

Ingredients

- 1 lb lean boneless lamb
- 1 tablespoon cooking oil
- 2 medium turnips, peeled and cut into 1/2 inch pieces
- 3 medium carrots, cut into 1/2 inch pieces
- 2 medium potatoes, cut into 1/2 inch pieces
- 2 medium onions, cut into wedges
- 1/4 cup quick-cooking tapioca
- 1/2 teaspoon salt
- 1/4 teaspoon pepper
- 1/4 teaspoon thyme
- 3 cups beef broth

Direction

- Cut the lamb into bite size cubes and brown it in the oil in a large skillet. Drain off the fat.
- Combine all ingredients in a slow cooker/crock pot. Cook on low for 6-8 hours or high 3-4 hours.

Nutrition Information

- Calories: 300.3
- Saturated Fat: 1.5
- Sodium: 1145
- Fiber: 5.7
- Sugar: 19.4
- Total Carbohydrate: 49.2
- Cholesterol: 23

- Total Fat: 6.4
- Protein: 12.9

38. Smoked Fish And Fresh Fruit

Serving: 12 units, 12 serving(s) | Prep: 20mins

Ingredients

- 7 ounces smoked salmon
- 7 ounces smoked trout
- 7 ounces smoked mackerel (or salt cod)
- 6 cherry tomatoes, halved
- 12 mixed green and red grapes, halved and deseeded
- 2 kiwi fruits, peeled and cut into 3/4-inch pieces
- 9 ounces assorted berries (strawberries, raspberries, etc)
- 6 green olives, pitted and halved
- fresh ground black pepper
- 1 lemon, quartered
- 12 skewers

Direction

- Cut the fish into 1-inch pieces.
- Alternate pieces of the three fish, folding where necessary, with the cherry tomatoes, fruit and olives.
- Season lightly with pepper and squeeze over the juice from the lemon wedges.

Nutrition Information

- Calories: 194.1
- Protein: 12.7
- Sodium: 186.9
- Sugar: 20.9
- Total Carbohydrate: 25.3
- Cholesterol: 28.7
- Total Fat: 5.6
- Saturated Fat: 1.2
- Fiber: 1.8

39. Southwestern Beef Chili With Corn

Serving: 4 serving(s) | Prep: 10mins | Cook: 20mins

Ingredients

- cooking spray
- 2 carrots, chopped
- 1 medium onion, chopped
- 1 garlic clove, minced
- 1/2 teaspoon salt
- 1/2 lb extra lean ground beef
- 2 tablespoons tomato paste
- 1 (4 ounce) can canned diced green chiles
- 2 (15 ounce) cans black beans, drained and rinsed
- 1 tablespoon chili powder
- 3 cups beef broth
- 1/2 cup corn kernel
- 1/2 cup cheddar cheese, grated
- 2 scallions, sliced

Direction

- Spray a large sauce pan and heat over medium high heat.
- Add the carrots, onion, garlic and salt and cook, stirring, for 3 minutes.
- Add the beef and cook, breaking it up with a spoon, until it is no longer pink, 3 to 5 minutes.
- Add the tomato paste and cook, stirring, until it is slightly darkened, 1 minute.
- Add the beans, green chiles, chili powder, beef broth, and 1/2 teaspoon salt.
- Simmer over medium heat until the vegetables are tender, about 10 minutes.
- Stir in the corn.
- Divide among bowls and top with the Cheddar and scallions.

Nutrition Information

- Calories: 411.5
- Sodium: 1066.6
- Fiber: 16.8
- Sugar: 3.9
- Protein: 32.8
- Total Fat: 9.6
- Saturated Fat: 4.6
- Total Carbohydrate: 51.2
- Cholesterol: 50.5

40. Spaghetti Agli E Olio

Serving: 2 serving(s) | Prep: 10mins | Cook: 10mins

Ingredients

- 200 g spaghetti
- 4 1/2 tablespoons extra virgin olive oil
- 6 garlic cloves, finely minced
- 1/2 teaspoon dried chili pepper flakes
- 1/2 cup fresh curly-leaf parsley, chopped
- 1/2 lemon, juice of
- salt and black pepper
- 1/2 cup parmesan cheese, grated to serve

Direction

- Cook pasta in boiling water with 1 tbsp. oil until al dente (or firm to bite), drain and keep warm. While pasta is cooking heat remaining oil in a small saucepan over a low heat. Add garlic and chili and cook 8 - 10 min, stirring often, until garlic is soft and slightly translucent. Add parsley and cook for 2 minutes. Remove from heat, add lemon juice and season with salt and pepper. Divide spaghetti among serving bowls, top with parsley mix, stir through and top with grated parmesan.

Nutrition Information

- Calories: 821.5
- Sodium: 398.8

- Cholesterol: 22
- Protein: 25.6
- Saturated Fat: 8.9
- Fiber: 4.4
- Sugar: 2.8
- Total Carbohydrate: 91.2
- Total Fat: 39.4

41. Spicy Garlic Grilled Shrimp

Serving: 4 serving(s) | Prep: 5mins | Cook: 6mins

Ingredients

- 16 large shrimp, shelled, deveined
- 1/2 cup olive oil
- 3 garlic cloves, coarsely chopped
- 2 tablespoons fresh oregano
- 2 tablespoons fresh flat leaf parsley
- 1 teaspoon red pepper flakes
- salt freshly ground black pepper

Direction

- In a medium bowl, combine the shrimp with the olive oil, garlic and oregano, parsley, red pepper flakes, and salt and pepper. Let marinate 1 hour.
- Remove shrimp from marinade and grill for 2 to 3 minutes on each side until cooked through.

Nutrition Information

- Calories: 267.4
- Total Fat: 27.4
- Saturated Fat: 3.8
- Sodium: 51.4
- Fiber: 0.4
- Sugar: 0.1
- Total Carbohydrate: 1.4
- Cholesterol: 42.9
- Protein: 4.9

42. Spicy Rice Filled Eggplant

Serving: 4 serving(s) | Prep: 30mins | Cook: 1hours

Ingredients

- 3/4 cup basmati rice
- 2 large eggplants
- 1 tablespoon olive oil
- 1 large brown onion, halved, finely chopped
- 1 red capsicum, halved, deseeded, finely chopped
- 2 garlic cloves, crushed
- 2 teaspoons ground coriander
- 1 teaspoon fresh ginger, finely grated
- 1/4 teaspoon chili, crushed
- 1/4 teaspoon ground turmeric
- 1/4 cup fresh flat leaf parsley, coarsely chopped
- 2 teaspoons lemon rind, finely grated
- 2 tablespoons fresh lemon juice
- 1/2 cup reduced-fat yoghurt
- 2 tablespoons of fresh mint, coarsely chopped

Direction

- Preheat oven to 200°C
- Cook the rice in a large saucepan of boiling water for 15 minutes or until tender. Rinse under cold running water. Drain well.
- Meanwhile, cut the eggplants in half lengthways and use a small sharp knife to cut a 1cm border around the edge of each eggplant half then scoop out the flesh within the border, leaving about 1.5cm of flesh on the base of each eggplant half.
- Finely chop the flesh.
- Heat oil in a frying pan over medium heat and add the onion and capsicum and cook, stirring, for 5 minutes or until soft.
- Add the garlic, coriander, ginger, chili and turmeric and cook, stirring, for 30 seconds or until aromatic.
- Add the chopped eggplant and cook, stirring, for 10 minutes or until eggplant is soft. Remove from heat.

- Add the rice, parsley, lemon rind and lemon juice to eggplant mixture, and stir to combine.
- Place eggplant shells in a large baking dish and spoon rice mixture evenly among eggplant shells.
- Bake in oven for 30 minutes or until eggplant shells are soft and filling is golden.
- Place the yoghurt and mint in a small serving bowl and stir to combine. Serve with spicy rice-filled eggplant.

Nutrition Information

- Calories: 277.2
- Total Fat: 6.3
- Saturated Fat: 1.5
- Fiber: 12.6
- Sugar: 11.3
- Cholesterol: 4
- Sodium: 29.3
- Total Carbohydrate: 51.9
- Protein: 7.7

43. Sweet Chilli Chicken Salad (21 Day Wonder Diet: Day 17)

Serving: 2 serving(s) | Prep: 15mins | Cook: 10mins

Ingredients

- 2 cups water
- 200 g chicken breast fillets
- 1 1/4 cups bean sprouts
- 1 small red capsicum, sliced thinly
- 1 small carrot, cut into matchsticks
- 1/4 cup lime juice
- 1 fresh long red fresh chili pepper, sliced thinly
- 1/3 cup fresh coriander leaves, firmly packed
- 15 g ginger, cut into matchsticks
- 1 tablespoon sweet chili sauce
- 2 teaspoons fish sauce

Direction

- Bring water to the boil in medium saucepan; add chicken. Simmer, covered, about 10 minutes or until chicken is cooked. Cool chicken in poaching liquid 10 minutes. Drain, and shred coarsely.
- Combine chicken in a medium bowl with sprout, capsicum, carrot, chili, coriander and ginger.
- Shake juice and sauces together in a screw top jar, drizzle over salad.

Nutrition Information

- Calories: 203.5
- Total Carbohydrate: 19.8
- Protein: 27.6
- Saturated Fat: 0.7
- Sodium: 610.5
- Fiber: 4.3
- Sugar: 7.7
- Total Fat: 2.4
- Cholesterol: 58.5

44. Theodore Kyriakou's Fricassee Of Green Dandelion Leaves

Serving: 6 serving(s) | Prep: 15mins | Cook: 1hours20mins

Ingredients

- 1 kg green dandelion greens, roots trimmed and washed well (if not available, look for curly endive leaves)
- 1 kg leek, trimmed, use white section only and discard tough outer leaves, rinsed well and cut into 2 . 5 cm pi
- 1 kg romaine lettuce, washed very well, and cut into 3 equal pieces
- 130 ml olive oil
- 1 small lemon, juice of
- 50 g dill, finely chopped
- sea salt, to taste
- fresh ground black pepper, to taste

Direction

- Drop the dandelion leaves or curly endive into a saucepan of boiling water and blanch with the lid on for 5 minutes.
- Drain the blanching water and put the dandelion leaves or endive back in the same pot.
- Add the leeks and 1 litre of boiling water.
- Place the lid back on the pot and cook over a medium heat for 20 minutes.
- Add the cos lettuce, mix everything well and put the lid back on.
- Continue cooking over the same heat for 40 minutes, by which time the leeks should be very tender and be falling apart and the vegetable broth should taste slightly sweet with a pleasant bitter after-taste (from the dandelion leaves).
- Season to taste, add the olive oil and cook for a further 15 minutes.
- Remove the pan from the heat and add the lemon juice and the chopped dill.
- Stir all the ingredients of the pot so that they are well-combined, transfer to a serving dish and serve.

Nutrition Information

- Calories: 376
- Sodium: 178.9
- Fiber: 12.5
- Total Carbohydrate: 45.6
- Protein: 9.4
- Total Fat: 21
- Saturated Fat: 3
- Sugar: 15.1
- Cholesterol: 0

45. Tilapia And Shrimp En Papollote

Serving: 1 serving(s) | Prep: 20mins | Cook: 9mins

Ingredients

- 1 (6 ounce) tilapia fillets
- 3 large raw shrimp, peeled and deveined
- 4 ounces vegetables, carrot, squash, and zucchini, julienned 1/4 inch wide by 4 inches long
- 1 ounce white wine or 1 ounce chicken stock or 1 ounce vegetable stock
- salt and pepper
- 1 tablespoon olive oil

Direction

- Preheat oven to 425°F
- Season vegetables with salt and pepper and toss with olive oil; mix well and set aside.
- Cut a large heart shape out of parchment paper and place on baking sheet or dish.
- Season tilapia and shrimp with salt and pepper on both sides.
- Place vegetables on one half of paper heart; top with tilapia and shrimp, and pour liquid on top of fish.
- Fold the empty half of the paper over the fish and vegetables; fold and crimp the edges of the paper to seal tightly. (Can be refrigerated now if you wish.).
- Bake for 7 to 9 minutes; the package should be puffy and the paper brown. (I had to cook mine significantly longer than this, so be prepared that it might take longer.).
- Place packet on a plate; cut open, being careful of the steam.

Nutrition Information

- Calories: 338.8
- Saturated Fat: 2.9
- Sodium: 121.8
- Sugar: 0.4
- Cholesterol: 117
- Total Fat: 16.8
- Fiber: 0
- Total Carbohydrate: 1.2
- Protein: 38.5

46. Tofu Dorowat

Serving: 6-8 serving(s) | Prep: 15mins | Cook: 1hours15mins

Ingredients

- 14 ounces crushed tomatoes
- 1 tablespoon paprika
- 1/2 cup dry red wine
- 1 tablespoon minced ginger
- 1/2 teaspoon ground cardamom
- 1/4 teaspoon nutmeg
- 1/3 teaspoon ground cloves
- 1/2 teaspoon cinnamon
- 1/3 teaspoon allspice
- 1 small onion, chopped fine
- 1 tablespoon minced garlic
- 2 tablespoons olive oil
- 1/2 teaspoon ground turmeric
- 700 g extra firm tofu, cut into cubes

Direction

- Mix tomatoes with paprika, 1/4 cup of wine, cardamom, nutmeg, cloves, cinnamon and allspice in a bowl, set aside.
- Sauté onions and garlic in a skillet with the oil.
- Add tomato sauce and tofu.
- Bring mixture to a boil, cover and simmer about 30 minutes.
- Uncover, add the other 1/4 cup of wine and simmer about 20 minutes.

Nutrition Information

- Calories: 169.1
- Protein: 10.5
- Total Fat: 9.8
- Saturated Fat: 1.7
- Fiber: 2.9
- Sugar: 3.9
- Cholesterol: 0
- Sodium: 158.3
- Total Carbohydrate: 9.7

47. Vegan Marinade (Marinated Tofu)

Serving: 4 serving(s) | Prep: 25mins

Ingredients

- 1/3 cup olive oil
- 1/3 cup balsamic vinegar
- 1/4 cup tamari
- 1 cup water
- 3 garlic cloves, crushed
- 8 basil leaves, chiffonade
- 1 teaspoon ground black pepper
- 2 (1 lb) packages firm tofu

Direction

- Stand the tofu up on end and cut down the middle, making two 1.5" slabs. Do this with both bricks of tofu and drain for at least 20 minutes, flipping halfway through. The longer you press the moisture out, the better the tofu will absorb the marinade.
- When the tofu has most of the water drained out, lay down in an 8x13 baking dish.
- Mix the ingredients for the marinade in a 2 cup (or more) measuring cup. Stir together well and pour over the tofu. Cover and set in the fridge for at least 1 hour, but for best results, marinade overnight, flipping at least once.
- Remove the tofu and press out the marinade with your hands as best you can.
- Here is where you can choose what to do with the tofu. It can be eaten cold, as is, on a sandwich. Baked on a greased cooking sheet at 400F until browned, then eaten as a "cutlet", chopped and tossed into a salad, or eaten as a hot sandwich. Same with frying it in a pan. Frying can give you a nice crust without drying out or firming up as much as when you bake it. Play with the options, food should be fun.

Nutrition Information

- Calories: 334.7
- Protein: 20.8
- Saturated Fat: 4.5
- Sodium: 1035.1
- Fiber: 2.6
- Sugar: 1.7
- Total Carbohydrate: 6.1
- Cholesterol: 0
- Total Fat: 27.5

48. Vegetable Stir Fry With Cashew Chilli

Serving: 4-6 serving(s) | Prep: 20mins | Cook: 5mins

Ingredients

- 4 tablespoons water
- 1 teaspoon garlic, crushed
- 100 g broccoli
- 100 g cauliflower
- 50 g mushrooms
- 2 carrots, sliced
- 2 red capsicums, sliced
- 125 g red cabbage, sliced
- 125 g snow peas
- 50 g sweet baby corn
- 1 tablespoon sweet chili sauce
- 1/2 cup roasted cashews

Direction

- Heat water in wok or non-stick fry pan and stir-fry crushed garlic and carrot over high heat, 2 to 3 minutes.
- Add all other vegs (cut the broccoli and cauliflower into florets) and stir-fry until just tender.
- Stir in sweet chili sauce.
- Scatter with cashews and serve with steamed rice or cooked noodles.
- Notes for Variation: For a chicken stir-fry, add 2 thinly sliced chicken fillets at the same time as the carrot.
- For more spice, add a teaspoon of chopped dried chili or 1/4 tsp of chili powder at the time you add the crushed garlic and carrot - watch out, it is hot!

Nutrition Information

- Calories: 178.5
- Sodium: 184.2
- Fiber: 5.7
- Total Carbohydrate: 22.6
- Protein: 6.7
- Total Fat: 8.7
- Saturated Fat: 1.7
- Sugar: 8.7
- Cholesterol: 0.3

49. Very Cheesy Macaroni And Cheese

Serving: 1-2 serving(s) | Prep: 2mins | Cook: 1mins

Ingredients

- 1 1/4 cups elbow macaroni, cooked but cooled
- 1 mozzarella string cheese
- 1 cup cheddar cheese
- 1/2 tablespoon butter
- 1 tablespoon milk
- 1 tablespoon parmesan cheese

Direction

- Put noodles in a microwave safe bowl.
- Add butter and milk.
- Chop the mozzarella stick into circles (about 1/4 inch), and grate the cheddar. Add the cheeses to the bowl.
- Microwave on high 1 1/2 minutes.
- Sprinkle grated parmesan cheese onto the macaroni and cheese.

- Enjoy!

Nutrition Information

- Calories: 1096.7
- Sodium: 1020
- Sugar: 4.5
- Protein: 54.6
- Total Fat: 51.7
- Saturated Fat: 31.9
- Fiber: 4.2
- Total Carbohydrate: 101.2
- Cholesterol: 158.6

50. Whole Grain Sesame Bread

Serving: 2 lb loaf, 20 serving(s) | Prep: 5mins | Cook: 25mins

Ingredients

- 1 1/4 cups buttermilk or 1 1/4 cups water
- 2 tablespoons butter
- 1 tablespoon sugar
- 1/4 cup honey
- 1/4 cup sesame seeds
- 2 tablespoons wheat germ
- 2 tablespoons nonfat dry milk powder
- 1 1/2 teaspoons salt
- 2 1/4 cups bread flour
- 1 cup whole wheat flour
- 3/4 cup rye flour
- 3 1/2 teaspoons bread machine yeast

Direction

- Add ingredients to bread machine in the order recommended by the manufacturer.
- Set Cycle: Whole Wheat, Size: 2lb.
- Check the dough after 5 minutes, add a tablespoon at a time of flour if too wet, or a tablespoon of water at a time if too dry.
- Dough should be smooth and slightly sticky to the touch.
- You may also remove the dough after kneading and bake in the oven at 350°F until well browned, about 25 minutes.

Nutrition Information

- Calories: 134.4
- Total Fat: 2.6
- Cholesterol: 3.8
- Protein: 4.2
- Saturated Fat: 1
- Sodium: 204.2
- Fiber: 2.1
- Sugar: 5.3
- Total Carbohydrate: 24.4

Index

A
ale 20
allspice 27
almond 3,4,12
anchovies 5
apple 3,11
apricot 3,6
artichoke 3,5,6
avocado 3,15,20

B
baking 13,14,17,25,26,27
balsamic vinegar 14,18,27
barbecue sauce 10
barley 3,16
basil 3,7,10,14,27
basmati rice 3,8,12,24
bay leaf 18
beans 13,23
beef 3,7,16,22,23
beer 9
berry 3,18
black beans 23
black pepper 5,6,7,8,9,14,15,16,21,22,23,24,25,27
bread 3,5,29
broccoli 28
broth 16,22,23,26
brown lentil 7
brown sugar 18
buns 15
burger 3,15
butter 3,7,8,9,16,18,19,21,28,29

C
cabbage 3,8,16
capers 5,7
capsicum 7,9,24,25,28
caramel 21
cardamom 12,27
carrot 4,9,22,23,25,26,28
cashew 3,28
cauliflower 28
cayenne pepper 9,13
celery 3,8,17,21
cheddar 23,28
cheese 3,6,7,11,19,23,28
cherry 7,16,22
chestnut 8
chicken 3,4,8,10,12,16,17,18,25,26,28
chickpea 3,10,11
chilli 3,25,28
chipotle 4
chips 15
chopped tomatoes 16
cinnamon 3,11,12,27
clarified butter 19
cloves 5,7,8,10,12,13,16,20,23,24,27
cod 3,13,22
coffee 3,14
coriander 24,25
cos lettuce 26
crackers 19
cream 3,11
crumble 7,17
cucumber 3,13,15
curry 12

D

dandelion 3,25,26

date 11

dijon mustard 13,15,17

dill 25,26

E

egg 1,3,4,8,24,25

F

falafel 16

fat 4,5,6,7,8,9,10,11,12,13,14,15,16,17,18,19,20,21,22,23,24,25,26,27,28,29

fennel 3,10,11

feta 7

fish 10,13,14,15,22,25,26

flour 16,17,21,29

fresh coriander 25

fruit 3,18,22

G

garam masala 10,11

garlic 3,5,7,8,10,11,12,13,14,15,16,17,20,21,23,24,27,28

ghee 18

gin 5,6,10,14,17,20,21,23,24,25,27

grain 3,12,15,29

grapefruit 3,20

grapes 22

green beans 4

H

hake 16,25

halibut 3,14

hare 2

heart 3,5,6,16,26

herbs 16

hoisin sauce 9

honey 17,29

I

ice cream 14

iceberg lettuce 7

J

jelly 18

jus 2,6,7,9,10,11,15,16,28

K

kiwi fruit 22

L

lamb 22

leek 25,26

lemon 4,5,6,9,11,12,13,14,16,18,20,22,23,24,25,26

lentils 7

lettuce 7,25

lime 6,7,25

ling 9,19,25,26

liqueur 14

M

macaroni 3,28

mace 19

margarine 8

mayonnaise 15

meat 3,7,18,19

milk 11,21,28,29

mince 5,13,14,15,20,21,23,27

mint 18,24,25

mixed berries 18

mozzarella 28

mushroom 15,16,20,28

mustard 14,15,17

N

noodles 28

nut 4,5,6,7,8,9,10,11,12,13,14,15,16,17,18,19,20,21,22,23,24,25,26,27,28,29

O

oil 4,5,6,7,8,9,10,11,12,13,14,15,16,17,18,19,20,21,22,23,24,25,26,27

olive 4,5,6,10,12,13,14,15,16,20,22,23,24,25,26,27

onion 3,4,7,8,9,12,16,18,21,22,23,24,27

orange 3,6,18

oregano 24

P

paprika 6,9,17,27

parmesan 23,28

parsley 5,13,14,16,23,24,25

pasta 3,4,7,19,23

peanut oil 12

pear 19

peas 3,4,13,19,28

peel 6,11,20,22,26

penne 4

pepper 3,4,5,6,7,8,9,10,11,13,14,15,16,17,18,19,20,21,22,23,24,25,26

pesto 3,4,19

pickle 13

pie 2,6,8,10,14,16,17,18,21,22,25

pineapple 11

plum 7

pork 3,9

port 2,3,15,19

potato 4,17,22

poultry 17

pulse 5

R

radish 6

red cabbage 8,28

red wine 5,16,27

redcurrant 18

rice 3,8,10,11,12,13,18,24,25,28

rosemary 9,15

rum 3,17

rye bread 19

rye flour 29

S

salad 3,6,13,15,18,19,25,27

salmon 3,20

salsa 3,14,15

salt 4,5,6,7,8,9,10,11,12,13,14,15,16,17,18,19,20,21,22,23,24,26,29

sauces 7,9,25

sausage 7

sea salt 7,16,25

seasoning 13,14,17

seeds 6

sesame oil 20

sesame seeds 29

sherry 21

shiitake mushroom 20

shin 13

smoked fish 3,22

smoked mackerel 22

smoked salmon 22

smoked trout 22

soba noodles 20

sorbet 3,11,12

soup 3,21

soy sauce 7,10,17,20

spaghetti 3,4,5,23

spinach 3,4,12,18

spring onion 7,9

squash 3,4,5,21,26

stew 3,4,16,22

stilton 3,19

stock 4,9,12,26

sugar 4,5,6,7,8,9,10,11,12,13,14,15,16,17,18,19,20,21,22,23,24,25,26,27,28,29

sweet potato 4

syrup 11

T

tamari 27

tapioca 22

tea 4,5,6,9,10,11,13,14,15,17,18,19,21,22,23,24,25,26,27,28,29

thai basil 10

thyme 9,21,22

tilapia 3,26

tofu 3,20,27

tomato 3,4,7,12,13,14,16,17,22,23,27

turmeric 24,27

turnip 22

V

vegan 3,27

vegetable oil 7,9,10,15

vegetable stock 26

vegetables 23,26

vinegar 5,14,18

W

walnut 3,11,19

water chestnut 3,8

white wine 26

wholemeal bread 19

wine 19,21,27

worcestershire sauce 16

Y

yeast 29

yoghurt 24,25

Z

zest 4

Conclusion

Thank you again for downloading this book!

I hope you enjoyed reading about my book!

If you enjoyed this book, please take the time to share your thoughts and post a review on Amazon. It'd be greatly appreciated!

Write me an honest review about the book – I truly value your opinion and thoughts and I will incorporate them into my next book, which is already underway.

Thank you!

If you have any questions, **feel free to contact at:** cookbook@lowpotassiumrecipes.com

David J. Patel

lowpotassiumrecipes.com

conversion chart
FOR THE KITCHEN

VOLUME MEASUREMENT CONVERSIONS

Cups	Tablespoons	Teaspoons	Milliliters
		1 tsp	5 ml
1/16 cup	1 tbsp	3 tsp	15 ml
1/8 cup	2 tbsp	6 tsp	30 ml
1/4 cup	4 tbsp	12 tsp	60 ml
1/3 cup	5 1/3 tbsp	16 tsp	80 ml
1/2 cup	8 tbsp	24 tsp	120 ml
2/3 cup	10 2/3 tbsp	32 tsp	160 ml
3/4 cup	12 tbsp	36 tsp	180 ml
1 cup	16 tbsp	48 tsp	240 ml

1 QUART =
2 pins
4 cups
32 ounces
950 ml

1 PINT =
2 cups
14 ounces
480 ml

1 CUP =
16 tbsp
8 ounces
240 ml

1/4 CUP =
4 tbsp
12 tsp
2 ounces
60 ml

1 TBSP =
3 tsp
1/2 ounce
15 ml

COOKING TEMPERATURE CONVERSIONS

Celcius/Centigrade   F = (Cx1.8) + 32
Fahrenheit   C = (F-32) x 0.5556

Recipe

Difficulty level:

o o O O O

Rating

♡ ♡ ♡ ♡ ♡

Prep Time:

Cooking Method:

Cooking Temp:

Cooking Time:

Servings:

Allergens:
- O Milk
- O Fish
- O Eggs
- O Lupin
- O Celery
- O Peanuts
- O Mustard
- O Molluscs
- O Tree nuts
- O Soybeans
- O Crustaceans
- O Sesame seeds
- O Cereals containing gluten
- O Sulphur dioxide and sulphites

Ingredients:

Cooking Instructions:

Notes:

Recipe

Difficulty level:

o o O O O

Rating

♡ ♡ ♡ ♡ ♡

Prep Time:

Cooking Method:

Cooking Temp:

Cooking Time:

Servings:

Allergens:
- O Milk
- O Fish
- O Eggs
- O Lupin
- O Celery
- O Peanuts
- O Mustard
- O Molluscs
- O Tree nuts
- O Soybeans
- O Crustaceans
- O Sesame seeds
- O Cereals containing gluten
- O Sulphur dioxide and sulphites

Ingredients:

Cooking Instructions:

Notes:

Recipe

Difficulty level:

○○○○○

Rating

♡♡♡♡♡

Prep Time:

Cooking Method:

Cooking Temp:

Cooking Time:

Servings:

Allergens:
- ○ Milk
- ○ Fish
- ○ Eggs
- ○ Lupin
- ○ Celery
- ○ Peanuts
- ○ Mustard
- ○ Molluscs
- ○ Tree nuts
- ○ Soybeans
- ○ Crustaceans
- ○ Sesame seeds
- ○ Cereals containing gluten
- ○ Sulphur dioxide and sulphites

Ingredients:

Cooking Instructions:

Notes:

Recipe

Difficulty level:

o o O O O

Rating

♡ ♡ ♡ ♡ ♥

Prep Time:

Cooking Method:

Cooking Temp:

Cooking Time:

Servings:

Allergens:

- O Milk
- O Fish
- O Eggs
- O Lupin
- O Celery
- O Peanuts
- O Mustard
- O Molluscs
- O Tree nuts
- O Soybeans
- O Crustaceans
- O Sesame seeds
- O Cereals containing gluten
- O Sulphur dioxide and sulphites

Ingredients:

Cooking Instructions:

Notes:

Recipe

Difficulty level:

o o O O O

Rating

♡ ♡ ♡ ♡ ♡

Prep Time:

Cooking Method:

Cooking Temp:

Cooking Time:

Servings:

Allergens:
- ○ Milk
- ○ Fish
- ○ Eggs
- ○ Lupin
- ○ Celery
- ○ Peanuts
- ○ Mustard
- ○ Molluscs
- ○ Tree nuts
- ○ Soybeans
- ○ Crustaceans
- ○ Sesame seeds
- ○ Cereals containing gluten
- ○ Sulphur dioxide and sulphites

Ingredients:

Cooking Instructions:

Notes:

Recipe

Difficulty level:

ooOOO

Rating

♡♡♡♡♥

Prep Time:

Cooking Method:

Cooking Temp:

Cooking Time:

Servings:

Allergens:
- O Milk
- O Fish
- O Eggs
- O Lupin
- O Celery
- O Peanuts
- O Mustard
- O Molluscs
- O Tree nuts
- O Soybeans
- O Crustaceans
- O Sesame seeds
- O Cereals containing gluten
- O Sulphur dioxide and sulphites

Ingredients:

Cooking Instructions:

Notes:

Recipe

Difficulty level:

ooOOO

Rating

♡ ♡ ♡ ♡ ♡

Prep Time:

Cooking Method:

Cooking Temp:

Cooking Time:

Servings:

Allergens:
- O Milk
- O Fish
- O Eggs
- O Lupin
- O Celery
- O Peanuts
- O Mustard
- O Molluscs
- O Tree nuts
- O Soybeans
- O Crustaceans
- O Sesame seeds
- O Cereals containing gluten
- O Sulphur dioxide and sulphites

Ingredients:

Cooking Instructions:

Notes:

Recipe

Difficulty level:

o o O O O

Rating

♡ ♡ ♡ ♡ ♡

Prep Time:

Cooking Method:

Cooking Temp:

Cooking Time:

Servings:

Allergens:
- O Milk
- O Fish
- O Eggs
- O Lupin
- O Celery
- O Peanuts
- O Mustard
- O Molluscs
- O Tree nuts
- O Soybeans
- O Crustaceans
- O Sesame seeds
- O Cereals containing gluten
- O Sulphur dioxide and sulphites

Ingredients:

Cooking Instructions:

Notes:

Recipe

Difficulty level:

o o O O O

Rating

♡ ♡ ♡ ♡ ♡

Prep Time:

Cooking Method:

Cooking Temp:

Cooking Time:

Servings:

Allergens:
- O Milk
- O Fish
- O Eggs
- O Lupin
- O Celery
- O Peanuts
- O Mustard
- O Molluscs
- O Tree nuts
- O Soybeans
- O Crustaceans
- O Sesame seeds
- O Cereals containing gluten
- O Sulphur dioxide and sulphites

Ingredients:

Cooking Instructions:

Notes:

Recipe

Difficulty level:

o o O O O

Rating

♡ ♡ ♡ ♡ ♡

Prep Time:

Cooking Method:

Cooking Temp:

Cooking Time:

Servings:

Allergens:
- O Milk
- O Fish
- O Eggs
- O Lupin
- O Celery
- O Peanuts
- O Mustard
- O Molluscs
- O Tree nuts
- O Soybeans
- O Crustaceans
- O Sesame seeds
- O Cereals containing gluten
- O Sulphur dioxide and sulphites

Ingredients:

Cooking Instructions:

Notes:

Recipe

Difficulty level:

ooOOO

Rating

♡♡♡♡♥

Prep Time:

Cooking Method:

Cooking Temp:

Cooking Time:

Servings:

Allergens:
- O Milk
- O Fish
- O Eggs
- O Lupin
- O Celery
- O Peanuts
- O Mustard
- O Molluscs
- O Tree nuts
- O Soybeans
- O Crustaceans
- O Sesame seeds
- O Cereals containing gluten
- O Sulphur dioxide and sulphites

Ingredients:

Cooking Instructions:

Notes:

Recipe

Difficulty level:

o o O O O

Rating

♡ ♡ ♡ ♡ ♡

Prep Time:

Cooking Method:

Cooking Temp:

Cooking Time:

Servings:

Allergens:

- O Milk
- O Fish
- O Eggs
- O Lupin
- O Celery
- O Peanuts
- O Mustard
- O Molluscs
- O Tree nuts
- O Soybeans
- O Crustaceans
- O Sesame seeds
- O Cereals containing gluten
- O Sulphur dioxide and sulphites

Ingredients:

Cooking Instructions:

Notes:

Recipe

Difficulty level:

o o O O O

Rating

♡ ♡ ♡ ♡ ♡

Prep Time:

Cooking Method:

Cooking Temp:

Cooking Time:

Servings:

Allergens:

- O Milk
- O Fish
- O Eggs
- O Lupin
- O Celery
- O Peanuts
- O Mustard
- O Molluscs
- O Tree nuts
- O Soybeans
- O Crustaceans
- O Sesame seeds
- O Cereals containing gluten
- O Sulphur dioxide and sulphites

Ingredients:

Cooking Instructions:

Notes:

Recipe

Difficulty level:

o o O O O

Rating

♡ ♡ ♡ ♡ ♡

Prep Time:

Cooking Method:

Cooking Temp:

Cooking Time:

Servings:

Allergens:
- O Milk
- O Fish
- O Eggs
- O Lupin
- O Celery
- O Peanuts
- O Mustard
- O Molluscs
- O Tree nuts
- O Soybeans
- O Crustaceans
- O Sesame seeds
- O Cereals containing gluten
- O Sulphur dioxide and sulphites

Ingredients:

Cooking Instructions:

Notes:

Recipe

Difficulty level:

o o O O O

Rating

♡ ♡ ♡ ♡ ♡

Prep Time:

Cooking Method:

Cooking Temp:

Cooking Time:

Servings:

Allergens:
- O Milk
- O Fish
- O Eggs
- O Lupin
- O Celery
- O Peanuts
- O Mustard
- O Molluscs
- O Tree nuts
- O Soybeans
- O Crustaceans
- O Sesame seeds
- O Cereals containing gluten
- O Sulphur dioxide and sulphites

Ingredients:

Cooking Instructions:

Notes:

Recipe

Difficulty level:

o o O O O

Rating

♡ ♡ ♡ ♡ ♡

Prep Time:

Cooking Method:

Cooking Temp:

Cooking Time:

Servings:

Allergens:
- O Milk
- O Fish
- O Eggs
- O Lupin
- O Celery
- O Peanuts
- O Mustard
- O Molluscs
- O Tree nuts
- O Soybeans
- O Crustaceans
- O Sesame seeds
- O Cereals containing gluten
- O Sulphur dioxide and sulphites

Ingredients:

Cooking Instructions:

Notes:

Recipe

Difficulty level:

o o O O O

Rating

♡ ♡ ♡ ♡ ♡

Prep Time:

Cooking Method:

Cooking Temp:

Cooking Time:

Servings:

Allergens:
- ○ Milk
- ○ Fish
- ○ Eggs
- ○ Lupin
- ○ Celery
- ○ Peanuts
- ○ Mustard
- ○ Molluscs
- ○ Tree nuts
- ○ Soybeans
- ○ Crustaceans
- ○ Sesame seeds
- ○ Cereals containing gluten
- ○ Sulphur dioxide and sulphites

Ingredients:

Cooking Instructions:

Notes:

Recipe

Difficulty level:

ooOOO

Rating

♡ ♡ ♡ ♡ ♡

Prep Time:

Cooking Method:

Cooking Temp:

Cooking Time:

Servings:

Allergens:
- O Milk
- O Fish
- O Eggs
- O Lupin
- O Celery
- O Peanuts
- O Mustard
- O Molluscs
- O Tree nuts
- O Soybeans
- O Crustaceans
- O Sesame seeds
- O Cereals containing gluten
- O Sulphur dioxide and sulphites

Ingredients:

Cooking Instructions:

Notes:

Recipe

Difficulty level:

ooOOO

Rating

♡♡♡♡♡

Prep Time:

Cooking Method:

Cooking Temp:

Cooking Time:

Servings:

Allergens:
- O Milk
- O Fish
- O Eggs
- O Lupin
- O Celery
- O Peanuts
- O Mustard
- O Molluscs
- O Tree nuts
- O Soybeans
- O Crustaceans
- O Sesame seeds
- O Cereals containing gluten
- O Sulphur dioxide and sulphites

Ingredients:

Cooking Instructions:

Notes:

Recipe

Difficulty level:

ooOOO

Rating

♡ ♡ ♡ ♡ ♥

Prep Time:

Cooking Method:

Cooking Temp:

Cooking Time:

Servings:

Allergens:

- O Milk
- O Fish
- O Eggs
- O Lupin
- O Celery
- O Peanuts
- O Mustard
- O Molluscs
- O Tree nuts
- O Soybeans
- O Crustaceans
- O Sesame seeds
- O Cereals containing gluten
- O Sulphur dioxide and sulphites

Ingredients:

Cooking Instructions:

Notes:

Recipe

Difficulty level:

○ ○ ○ ○ ○

Rating

♡ ♡ ♡ ♡ ♡

Prep Time:

Cooking Method:

Cooking Temp:

Cooking Time:

Servings:

Allergens:

- ○ Milk
- ○ Fish
- ○ Eggs
- ○ Lupin
- ○ Celery
- ○ Peanuts
- ○ Mustard
- ○ Molluscs
- ○ Tree nuts
- ○ Soybeans
- ○ Crustaceans
- ○ Sesame seeds
- ○ Cereals containing gluten
- ○ Sulphur dioxide and sulphites

Ingredients:

Cooking Instructions:

Notes:

Recipe

Difficulty level:

o o O O O

Rating

♡ ♡ ♡ ♡ ♡

Prep Time:

Cooking Method:

Cooking Temp:

Cooking Time:

Servings:

Allergens:
- O Milk
- O Fish
- O Eggs
- O Lupin
- O Celery
- O Peanuts
- O Mustard
- O Molluscs
- O Tree nuts
- O Soybeans
- O Crustaceans
- O Sesame seeds
- O Cereals containing gluten
- O Sulphur dioxide and sulphites

Ingredients:

Cooking Instructions:

Notes:

Recipe

Difficulty level:

ooOOO

Rating

♡♡♡♥♥

Prep Time:

Cooking Method:

Cooking Temp:

Cooking Time:

Servings:

Allergens:
- O Milk
- O Fish
- O Eggs
- O Lupin
- O Celery
- O Peanuts
- O Mustard
- O Molluscs
- O Tree nuts
- O Soybeans
- O Crustaceans
- O Sesame seeds
- O Cereals containing gluten
- O Sulphur dioxide and sulphites

Ingredients:

Cooking Instructions:

Notes:

Recipe

Difficulty level:

o o O O O

Rating

♡ ♡ ♡ ♡ ♡

Prep Time:

Cooking Method:

Cooking Temp:

Cooking Time:

Servings:

Allergens:

- O Milk
- O Fish
- O Eggs
- O Lupin
- O Celery
- O Peanuts
- O Mustard
- O Molluscs
- O Tree nuts
- O Soybeans
- O Crustaceans
- O Sesame seeds
- O Cereals containing gluten
- O Sulphur dioxide and sulphites

Ingredients:

Cooking Instructions:

Notes:

Recipe

Difficulty level:

o o O O O

Rating

♡ ♡ ♡ ♡ ♡

Prep Time:

Cooking Method:

Cooking Temp:

Cooking Time:

Servings:

Allergens:
- O Milk
- O Fish
- O Eggs
- O Lupin
- O Celery
- O Peanuts
- O Mustard
- O Molluscs
- O Tree nuts
- O Soybeans
- O Crustaceans
- O Sesame seeds
- O Cereals containing gluten
- O Sulphur dioxide and sulphites

Ingredients:

Cooking Instructions:

Notes:

Recipe

Difficulty level:

o o O O O

Rating

♡ ♡ ♡ ♡ ♡

Prep Time:

Cooking Method:

Cooking Temp:

Cooking Time:

Servings:

Allergens:
- O Milk
- O Fish
- O Eggs
- O Lupin
- O Celery
- O Peanuts
- O Mustard
- O Molluscs
- O Tree nuts
- O Soybeans
- O Crustaceans
- O Sesame seeds
- O Cereals containing gluten
- O Sulphur dioxide and sulphites

Ingredients:

Cooking Instructions:

Notes:

Recipe

Difficulty level:

o o O O O

Rating

♡ ♡ ♡ ♡ ♡

Prep Time:

Cooking Method:

Cooking Temp:

Cooking Time:

Servings:

Allergens:
- O Milk
- O Fish
- O Eggs
- O Lupin
- O Celery
- O Peanuts
- O Mustard
- O Molluscs
- O Tree nuts
- O Soybeans
- O Crustaceans
- O Sesame seeds
- O Cereals containing gluten
- O Sulphur dioxide and sulphites

Ingredients:

Cooking Instructions:

Notes:

Recipe

Difficulty level:

ooOOO

Rating

♡ ♡ ♡ ♡ ♥

Prep Time:

Cooking Method:

Cooking Temp:

Cooking Time:

Servings:

Allergens:
- O Milk
- O Fish
- O Eggs
- O Lupin
- O Celery
- O Peanuts
- O Mustard
- O Molluscs
- O Tree nuts
- O Soybeans
- O Crustaceans
- O Sesame seeds
- O Cereals containing gluten
- O Sulphur dioxide and sulphites

Ingredients:

Cooking Instructions:

Notes:

Recipe

Difficulty level:

o o O O O

Rating

♡ ♡ ♡ ♡ ♡

Prep Time:

Cooking Method:

Cooking Temp:

Cooking Time:

Servings:

Allergens:
- O Milk
- O Fish
- O Eggs
- O Lupin
- O Celery
- O Peanuts
- O Mustard
- O Molluscs
- O Tree nuts
- O Soybeans
- O Crustaceans
- O Sesame seeds
- O Cereals containing gluten
- O Sulphur dioxide and sulphites

Ingredients:

Cooking Instructions:

Notes:

Recipe

Difficulty level:

o o O O O

Rating

♡ ♡ ♡ ♡ ♡

Prep Time:

Cooking Method:

Cooking Temp:

Cooking Time:

Servings:

Allergens:
- O Milk
- O Fish
- O Eggs
- O Lupin
- O Celery
- O Peanuts
- O Mustard
- O Molluscs
- O Tree nuts
- O Soybeans
- O Crustaceans
- O Sesame seeds
- O Cereals containing gluten
- O Sulphur dioxide and sulphites

Ingredients:

Cooking Instructions:

Notes:

Recipe

Difficulty level:

○ ○ ○ ○ ○

Rating

♡ ♡ ♡ ♡ ♡

Prep Time:

Cooking Method:

Cooking Temp:

Cooking Time:

Servings:

Allergens:
- ○ Milk
- ○ Fish
- ○ Eggs
- ○ Lupin
- ○ Celery
- ○ Peanuts
- ○ Mustard
- ○ Molluscs
- ○ Tree nuts
- ○ Soybeans
- ○ Crustaceans
- ○ Sesame seeds
- ○ Cereals containing gluten
- ○ Sulphur dioxide and sulphites

Ingredients:

Cooking Instructions:

Notes:

Recipe

Difficulty level:

o o O O O

Rating

♡ ♡ ♡ ♡ ♡

Prep Time:

Cooking Method:

Cooking Temp:

Cooking Time:

Servings:

Allergens:
- O Milk
- O Fish
- O Eggs
- O Lupin
- O Celery
- O Peanuts
- O Mustard
- O Molluscs
- O Tree nuts
- O Soybeans
- O Crustaceans
- O Sesame seeds
- O Cereals containing gluten
- O Sulphur dioxide and sulphites

Ingredients:

Cooking Instructions:

Notes:

Recipe

Difficulty level:

ooOOO

Rating

♡ ♡ ♡ ♡ ♡

Prep Time:

Cooking Method:

Cooking Temp:

Cooking Time:

Servings:

Allergens:

- O Milk
- O Fish
- O Eggs
- O Lupin
- O Celery
- O Peanuts
- O Mustard
- O Molluscs
- O Tree nuts
- O Soybeans
- O Crustaceans
- O Sesame seeds
- O Cereals containing gluten
- O Sulphur dioxide and sulphites

Ingredients:

Cooking Instructions:

Notes:

Recipe

Difficulty level:

o o O O O

Rating

♡ ♡ ♡ ♡ ♡

Prep Time:

Cooking Method:

Cooking Temp:

Cooking Time:

Servings:

Allergens:
- O Milk
- O Fish
- O Eggs
- O Lupin
- O Celery
- O Peanuts
- O Mustard
- O Molluscs
- O Tree nuts
- O Soybeans
- O Crustaceans
- O Sesame seeds
- O Cereals containing gluten
- O Sulphur dioxide and sulphites

Ingredients:

Cooking Instructions:

Notes:

Recipe

Difficulty level:

o o O O O

Rating

♡ ♡ ♡ ♡ ♡

Prep Time:

Cooking Method:

Cooking Temp:

Cooking Time:

Servings:

Allergens:
- O Milk
- O Fish
- O Eggs
- O Lupin
- O Celery
- O Peanuts
- O Mustard
- O Molluscs
- O Tree nuts
- O Soybeans
- O Crustaceans
- O Sesame seeds
- O Cereals containing gluten
- O Sulphur dioxide and sulphites

Ingredients:

Cooking Instructions:

Notes:

Recipe

Difficulty level:

o o O O O

Rating

♡ ♡ ♡ ♡ ♡

Prep Time:

Cooking Method:

Cooking Temp:

Cooking Time:

Servings:

Allergens:
- O Milk
- O Fish
- O Eggs
- O Lupin
- O Celery
- O Peanuts
- O Mustard
- O Molluscs
- O Tree nuts
- O Soybeans
- O Crustaceans
- O Sesame seeds
- O Cereals containing gluten
- O Sulphur dioxide and sulphites

Ingredients:

Cooking Instructions:

Notes:

Recipe

Difficulty level:

ooOOO

Rating

♡♡♡♡♥

Prep Time:

Cooking Method:

Cooking Temp:

Cooking Time:

Servings:

Allergens:
- O Milk
- O Fish
- O Eggs
- O Lupin
- O Celery
- O Peanuts
- O Mustard
- O Molluscs
- O Tree nuts
- O Soybeans
- O Crustaceans
- O Sesame seeds
- O Cereals containing gluten
- O Sulphur dioxide and sulphites

Ingredients:

Cooking Instructions:

Notes:

Recipe

Difficulty level:

o o O O O

Rating

♡ ♡ ♡ ♡ ♡

Prep Time:

Cooking Method:

Cooking Temp:

Cooking Time:

Servings:

Allergens:
- ○ Milk
- ○ Fish
- ○ Eggs
- ○ Lupin
- ○ Celery
- ○ Peanuts
- ○ Mustard
- ○ Molluscs
- ○ Tree nuts
- ○ Soybeans
- ○ Crustaceans
- ○ Sesame seeds
- ○ Cereals containing gluten
- ○ Sulphur dioxide and sulphites

Ingredients:

Cooking Instructions:

Notes:

Recipe

Difficulty level:
o o O O O

Rating
♡ ♡ ♡ ♡ ♡

Prep Time:

Cooking Method:

Cooking Temp:

Cooking Time:

Servings:

Allergens:
- O Milk
- O Fish
- O Eggs
- O Lupin
- O Celery
- O Peanuts
- O Mustard
- O Molluscs
- O Tree nuts
- O Soybeans
- O Crustaceans
- O Sesame seeds
- O Cereals containing gluten
- O Sulphur dioxide and sulphites

Ingredients:

Cooking Instructions:

Notes:

Recipe

Difficulty level:

o o O O O

Rating

♡ ♡ ♡ ♥ ♥

Prep Time:

Cooking Method:

Cooking Temp:

Cooking Time:

Servings:

Allergens:
- O Milk
- O Fish
- O Eggs
- O Lupin
- O Celery
- O Peanuts
- O Mustard
- O Molluscs
- O Tree nuts
- O Soybeans
- O Crustaceans
- O Sesame seeds
- O Cereals containing gluten
- O Sulphur dioxide and sulphites

Ingredients:

Cooking Instructions:

Notes:

Recipe

Difficulty level:

o o O O O

Rating

♡ ♡ ♡ ♡ ♡

Prep Time:

Cooking Method:

Cooking Temp:

Cooking Time:

Servings:

Allergens:
- O Milk
- O Fish
- O Eggs
- O Lupin
- O Celery
- O Peanuts
- O Mustard
- O Molluscs
- O Tree nuts
- O Soybeans
- O Crustaceans
- O Sesame seeds
- O Cereals containing gluten
- O Sulphur dioxide and sulphites

Ingredients:

Cooking Instructions:

Notes:

Recipe

Difficulty level:

o o O O O

Rating

♡ ♡ ♡ ♡ ♡

Prep Time:

Cooking Method:

Cooking Temp:

Cooking Time:

Servings:

Allergens:
- O Milk
- O Fish
- O Eggs
- O Lupin
- O Celery
- O Peanuts
- O Mustard
- O Molluscs
- O Tree nuts
- O Soybeans
- O Crustaceans
- O Sesame seeds
- O Cereals containing gluten
- O Sulphur dioxide and sulphites

Ingredients:

Cooking Instructions:

Notes:

Recipe

Difficulty level:

o o O O O

Rating

♡ ♡ ♡ ♡ ♡

Prep Time:

Cooking Method:

Cooking Temp:

Cooking Time:

Servings:

Allergens:
- Milk
- Fish
- Eggs
- Lupin
- Celery
- Peanuts
- Mustard
- Molluscs
- Tree nuts
- Soybeans
- Crustaceans
- Sesame seeds
- Cereals containing gluten
- Sulphur dioxide and sulphites

Ingredients:

Cooking Instructions:

Notes:

Recipe

Difficulty level:

o o O O O

Rating

♡ ♡ ♡ ♡ ♡

Prep Time:

Cooking Method:

Cooking Temp:

Cooking Time:

Servings:

Allergens:

- O Milk
- O Fish
- O Eggs
- O Lupin
- O Celery
- O Peanuts
- O Mustard
- O Molluscs
- O Tree nuts
- O Soybeans
- O Crustaceans
- O Sesame seeds
- O Cereals containing gluten
- O Sulphur dioxide and sulphites

Ingredients:

Cooking Instructions:

Notes:

Recipe

Difficulty level:

ooOOO

Rating

♡♡♡♡♥

Prep Time:

Cooking Method:

Cooking Temp:

Cooking Time:

Servings:

Allergens:
- ○ Milk
- ○ Fish
- ○ Eggs
- ○ Lupin
- ○ Celery
- ○ Peanuts
- ○ Mustard
- ○ Molluscs
- ○ Tree nuts
- ○ Soybeans
- ○ Crustaceans
- ○ Sesame seeds
- ○ Cereals containing gluten
- ○ Sulphur dioxide and sulphites

Ingredients:

Cooking Instructions:

Notes:

Recipe

Difficulty level:

o o O O O

Rating

♡ ♡ ♡ ♡ ♡

Prep Time:

Cooking Method:

Cooking Temp:

Cooking Time:

Servings:

Allergens:
- O Milk
- O Fish
- O Eggs
- O Lupin
- O Celery
- O Peanuts
- O Mustard
- O Molluscs
- O Tree nuts
- O Soybeans
- O Crustaceans
- O Sesame seeds
- O Cereals containing gluten
- O Sulphur dioxide and sulphites

Ingredients:

Cooking Instructions:

Notes:

Recipe

Difficulty level:

o o O O O

Rating

♡ ♡ ♡ ♡ ♡

Prep Time:

Cooking Method:

Cooking Temp:

Cooking Time:

Servings:

Allergens:
- O Milk
- O Fish
- O Eggs
- O Lupin
- O Celery
- O Peanuts
- O Mustard
- O Molluscs
- O Tree nuts
- O Soybeans
- O Crustaceans
- O Sesame seeds
- O Cereals containing gluten
- O Sulphur dioxide and sulphites

Ingredients:

Cooking Instructions:

Notes:

Recipe

Difficulty level:

o o O O O

Rating

♡ ♡ ♡ ♡ ♡

Prep Time:

Cooking Method:

Cooking Temp:

Cooking Time:

Servings:

Allergens:

- O Milk
- O Fish
- O Eggs
- O Lupin
- O Celery
- O Peanuts
- O Mustard
- O Molluscs
- O Tree nuts
- O Soybeans
- O Crustaceans
- O Sesame seeds
- O Cereals containing gluten
- O Sulphur dioxide and sulphites

Ingredients:

Cooking Instructions:

Notes:

Recipe

Difficulty level:

o o O O O

Rating

♡ ♡ ♡ ♡ ♡

Prep Time:

Cooking Method:

Cooking Temp:

Cooking Time:

Servings:

Allergens:
- O Milk
- O Fish
- O Eggs
- O Lupin
- O Celery
- O Peanuts
- O Mustard
- O Molluscs
- O Tree nuts
- O Soybeans
- O Crustaceans
- O Sesame seeds
- O Cereals containing gluten
- O Sulphur dioxide and sulphites

Ingredients:

Cooking Instructions:

Notes:

Recipe

Difficulty level:

o o O O O

Rating

♡ ♡ ♡ ♡ ♡

Prep Time:

Cooking Method:

Cooking Temp:

Cooking Time:

Servings:

Allergens:
- O Milk
- O Fish
- O Eggs
- O Lupin
- O Celery
- O Peanuts
- O Mustard
- O Molluscs
- O Tree nuts
- O Soybeans
- O Crustaceans
- O Sesame seeds
- O Cereals containing gluten
- O Sulphur dioxide and sulphites

Ingredients:

Cooking Instructions:

Notes:

Recipe

Difficulty level:

ooOOO

Rating

♡ ♡ ♡ ♡ ♡

Prep Time:

Cooking Method:

Cooking Temp:

Cooking Time:

Servings:

Allergens:
- O Milk
- O Fish
- O Eggs
- O Lupin
- O Celery
- O Peanuts
- O Mustard
- O Molluscs
- O Tree nuts
- O Soybeans
- O Crustaceans
- O Sesame seeds
- O Cereals containing gluten
- O Sulphur dioxide and sulphites

Ingredients:

Cooking Instructions:

Notes:

Recipe

Difficulty level:

o o O O O

Rating

♡ ♡ ♡ ♡ ♡

Prep Time:

Cooking Method:

Cooking Temp:

Cooking Time:

Servings:

Allergens:
- O Milk
- O Fish
- O Eggs
- O Lupin
- O Celery
- O Peanuts
- O Mustard
- O Molluscs
- O Tree nuts
- O Soybeans
- O Crustaceans
- O Sesame seeds
- O Cereals containing gluten
- O Sulphur dioxide and sulphites

Ingredients:

Cooking Instructions:

Notes:

Recipe

Difficulty level:

o o O O O

Rating

♡ ♡ ♡ ♡ ♡

Prep Time:

Cooking Method:

Cooking Temp:

Cooking Time:

Servings:

Allergens:
- Milk
- Fish
- Eggs
- Lupin
- Celery
- Peanuts
- Mustard
- Molluscs
- Tree nuts
- Soybeans
- Crustaceans
- Sesame seeds
- Cereals containing gluten
- Sulphur dioxide and sulphites

Ingredients:

Cooking Instructions:

Notes:

Recipe

Difficulty level:

o o O O O

Rating

♡ ♡ ♡ ♡ ♡

Prep Time:

Cooking Method:

Cooking Temp:

Cooking Time:

Servings:

Allergens:

- O Milk
- O Fish
- O Eggs
- O Lupin
- O Celery
- O Peanuts
- O Mustard
- O Molluscs
- O Tree nuts
- O Soybeans
- O Crustaceans
- O Sesame seeds
- O Cereals containing gluten
- O Sulphur dioxide and sulphites

Ingredients:

Cooking Instructions:

Notes:

Recipe

Difficulty level:

ooOOO

Rating

♡♡♡♡♡

Prep Time:

Cooking Method:

Cooking Temp:

Cooking Time:

Servings:

Allergens:
- ○ Milk
- ○ Fish
- ○ Eggs
- ○ Lupin
- ○ Celery
- ○ Peanuts
- ○ Mustard
- ○ Molluscs
- ○ Tree nuts
- ○ Soybeans
- ○ Crustaceans
- ○ Sesame seeds
- ○ Cereals containing gluten
- ○ Sulphur dioxide and sulphites

Ingredients:

Cooking Instructions:

Notes:

Recipe

Difficulty level:

ooOOO

Rating

♡ ♡ ♡ ♡ ♡

Prep Time:

Cooking Method:

Cooking Temp:

Cooking Time:

Servings:

Allergens:

- O Milk
- O Fish
- O Eggs
- O Lupin
- O Celery
- O Peanuts
- O Mustard
- O Molluscs
- O Tree nuts
- O Soybeans
- O Crustaceans
- O Sesame seeds
- O Cereals containing gluten
- O Sulphur dioxide and sulphites

Ingredients:

Cooking Instructions:

Notes:

Recipe

Difficulty level:

o o O O O

Rating

♡ ♡ ♡ ♡ ♡

Prep Time:

Cooking Method:

Cooking Temp:

Cooking Time:

Servings:

Allergens:

- O Milk
- O Fish
- O Eggs
- O Lupin
- O Celery
- O Peanuts
- O Mustard
- O Molluscs
- O Tree nuts
- O Soybeans
- O Crustaceans
- O Sesame seeds
- O Cereals containing gluten
- O Sulphur dioxide and sulphites

Ingredients:

Cooking Instructions:

Notes:

Recipe

Difficulty level:

o o O O O

Rating

♡ ♡ ♡ ♡ ♥

Prep Time:

Cooking Method:

Cooking Temp:

Cooking Time:

Servings:

Allergens:
- O Milk
- O Fish
- O Eggs
- O Lupin
- O Celery
- O Peanuts
- O Mustard
- O Molluscs
- O Tree nuts
- O Soybeans
- O Crustaceans
- O Sesame seeds
- O Cereals containing gluten
- O Sulphur dioxide and sulphites

Ingredients:

Cooking Instructions:

Notes:

Recipe

Difficulty level:

ooOOO

Rating

♡♡♡♡♡

Prep Time:

Cooking Method:

Cooking Temp:

Cooking Time:

Servings:

Allergens:
- O Milk
- O Fish
- O Eggs
- O Lupin
- O Celery
- O Peanuts
- O Mustard
- O Molluscs
- O Tree nuts
- O Soybeans
- O Crustaceans
- O Sesame seeds
- O Cereals containing gluten
- O Sulphur dioxide and sulphites

Ingredients:

Cooking Instructions:

Notes:

Recipe

Difficulty level:

ooOOO

Rating

♡♡♡♡♡

Prep Time:

Cooking Method:

Cooking Temp:

Cooking Time:

Servings:

Allergens:
- O Milk
- O Fish
- O Eggs
- O Lupin
- O Celery
- O Peanuts
- O Mustard
- O Molluscs
- O Tree nuts
- O Soybeans
- O Crustaceans
- O Sesame seeds
- O Cereals containing gluten
- O Sulphur dioxide and sulphites

Ingredients:

Cooking Instructions:

Notes:

Recipe

Difficulty level:

○○○○○

Rating

♡♡♡♡♡

Prep Time:

Cooking Method:

Cooking Temp:

Cooking Time:

Servings:

Allergens:
- ○ Milk
- ○ Fish
- ○ Eggs
- ○ Lupin
- ○ Celery
- ○ Peanuts
- ○ Mustard
- ○ Molluscs
- ○ Tree nuts
- ○ Soybeans
- ○ Crustaceans
- ○ Sesame seeds
- ○ Cereals containing gluten
- ○ Sulphur dioxide and sulphites

Ingredients:

Cooking Instructions:

Notes:

Recipe

Difficulty level:

o o O O O

Rating

♡ ♡ ♡ ♡ ♡

Prep Time:

Cooking Method:

Cooking Temp:

Cooking Time:

Servings:

Allergens:
- O Milk
- O Fish
- O Eggs
- O Lupin
- O Celery
- O Peanuts
- O Mustard
- O Molluscs
- O Tree nuts
- O Soybeans
- O Crustaceans
- O Sesame seeds
- O Cereals containing gluten
- O Sulphur dioxide and sulphites

Ingredients:

Cooking Instructions:

Notes:

Recipe

Difficulty level:

o o O O O

Rating

♡ ♡ ♡ ♡ ♡

Prep Time:

Cooking Method:

Cooking Temp:

Cooking Time:

Servings:

Allergens:

- O Milk
- O Fish
- O Eggs
- O Lupin
- O Celery
- O Peanuts
- O Mustard
- O Molluscs
- O Tree nuts
- O Soybeans
- O Crustaceans
- O Sesame seeds
- O Cereals containing gluten
- O Sulphur dioxide and sulphites

Ingredients:

Cooking Instructions:

Notes:

Recipe

Difficulty level:

ooOOO

Rating

♡♡♡♡♡

Prep Time:

Cooking Method:

Cooking Temp:

Cooking Time:

Servings:

Allergens:

- O Milk
- O Fish
- O Eggs
- O Lupin
- O Celery
- O Peanuts
- O Mustard
- O Molluscs
- O Tree nuts
- O Soybeans
- O Crustaceans
- O Sesame seeds
- O Cereals containing gluten
- O Sulphur dioxide and sulphites

Ingredients:

Cooking Instructions:

Notes: